Graphic Representation
of Models
in Linguistic Theory

Graphic Representation of Models in Linguistic Theory

ANN HARLEMAN STEWART

Indiana University Press
Bloomington & London

Published in Canada by Fitzhenry & Whiteside Limited,
Don Mills, Ontario

Manufactured in the United States of America

Library of Congress Cataloging in Publication Data

Stewart, Ann Harleman.
    Graphic representation of models in linguistic
theory.

    Bibliography.
    Includes index.
    1. Linguistics--Graphic methods. 2. Linguistic
models. I. Title.
P123.S685   410'.1'84   75-5285
ISBN 0-253-32624-9   1 2 3 4 5 80 79 78 77 76

Contents

Acknowledgments

I would like to thank the following scholars for their comments on earlier versions of this work: Hans C. Arsleff, Sonja Bargmann, Harold C. Conklin, David W. Crabb, Murray Fowler, Albert H. Marckwardt, William G. Moulton, and Irving Zaretsky. I am indebted as well to many other scholars in various fields--too many to list here--for their suggestions.

I would like to thank also Princeton University, the Institute for Research in the Humanities of the University of Wisconsin, and the University of Washington for financial support during the writing of this work.

I am especially grateful to Betty Johnson, graphic designer and typist for this book, for her painstaking attention and her humor.

Graphic Representation
of Models
in Linguistic Theory

Introduction

Sometimes the same thing is not
even synonymous with itself.
--Y. R. Chao

The first thing that is necessary for an analysis of graphic representation in linguistics is a definition of graphic representation in linguistics. In this book, the term "graphic representation" embraces most, though by no means all, of the figures or diagrams that are used in linguistics, and that are graphic. "Graphic" rules out not only prose description (Hockett's [1947] formulation of the item-and-arrangement and item-and-process models of grammar, for example), but also mathematical notation and systems of representation that involve concatenations of symbols rather than diagrams. Thus the reader will not find here any treatment of mathematical models in linguistics, nor any application of mathematical techniques (such as graph theory or calculus) to linguistic concepts, beyond the rudimentary mathematics necessary (as in Chapter 6) to illuminate a particular *graphic* device. Again, the reader will not find here any treatment of systems of representation that concatenate symbols--themselves a kind of mathematics, an algebra--such as the systems of categorial grammar or tagmemic analysis.

Even within these limits, this work is not meant to be exhaustive. Every sort of diagram current in linguistics could not possibly be included.

For instance, the graphic representation used for
stratificational grammar, as well as that used for
systemic linguistics--both greatly modified tree
diagrams--is not discussed in great detail, though
the tree diagram itself, of course, is. The diagrams that *are* included are included because they
illustrate the approach to linguistics taken in
this book. Some, like the tree diagrams for immediate constituent analysis, represent major
theoretical trends; others, like the matrix for
Bell's Visible Speech, while comparatively minor
elements in linguistics as a whole, serve to make
a particular point--the provenience of a figure,
for example, or its spread over various schools
of linguistics. The diagrams included here, then,
constitute a selection from, not a collection of,
the diagrams in current use in linguistics.

     "Representation," the other half of the term,
requires that the figures or diagrams be used to
represent something; that they make statements
about the world; that they have meaning. Accordingly, we can divide graphic representation into
form and meaning. We can separate the figure,
whatever it is--say, a tree diagram--from the
meaning it conveys in a given instance--say, immediate constituent analysis. This dichotomy between form and meaning makes possible the taxonomy
of figures in linguistics that comprises the first
three chapters of this book. It is a taxonomy of
figures on the basis of graphic criteria into three
types--tree diagrams, matrix diagrams, and box
diagrams--and a discussion of the meanings for
which the three types stand. It, too, is not exhaustive; it is meant, not as a comprehensive survey of the figures in use in linguistics, but as
a demonstration of the feasibility of the approach
taken in this book to the problem posed by the
graphic representation of models in linguistic
theory.

     The problem lies in the existence of homonymy
and synonymy: most of the figures can stand for
more than one meaning, and most of the meanings
can be expressed by more than one figure. When

one looks at any given diagram, therefore, one cannot know, when faced with a tree diagram, for instance, whether it sets out the data in a family
tree, in a taxonomy, in a componential analysis,
or in an immediate constituent analysis. One cannot know until he looks at the data and at the context of the work in which the diagram appears and
infers the statement that the diagram is making:
if the figure appears in a work on historical linguistics and the data are the names of languages,
its meaning must be a genealogy of the data; if
the figure appears in a work on syntax and the
data are words, its meaning is probably the immediate constituent analysis of the data; and so on.
In short, the process by which diagrams in linguistics are interpreted is a process of circular reasoning. Using diagrams to make statements about
the data amounts to begging the question.

So it is that graphic representation in linguistics is a thing sometimes not even synonymous
with itself. As things stand, linguistics takes
with respect to diagrams the position of Humpty
Dumpty on words. "When I use a word," says Lewis
Carroll's character, "it means just what *I* choose
it to mean--neither more nor less; to which Alice
sensibly responds with the question, "whether you
can make words mean so many different things." It
is not only that you cannot do so except at the
price of circular reasoning, at the price of
draining all the various figures of meaning, so
that they are ready at any moment to mean what
their users choose them to mean. It is also a
matter of the influence of graphic representation
on the development of linguistic theory--an influence, as things stand now, that is neither
governed nor allowed for.

The mere possibility of a taxonomy of figures suggests the weight of graphic representation
in linguistic science. It suggests as well the
autonomy of graphic representation in linguistic
science; for our classification, which proceeds
by what we might call graphic least common denom-
inators, cuts across other classifications of

linguistic theory--by period, by type of theory
(structural *versus* transformational), by subject
phonology *versus* morphology). Thus we should not
be surprised to find that a figure can come to
have a life of its own, to influence the theory
out of which it grew. In looking, in Chapter 4,
at examples of graphic representation having directed the development of linguistic theory, we
will take the first of two perspectives on the
subject. From this vantage point, the vantage
point of the philosophy of science, we view graphic representation as a component of linguistic
science, as occupying in linguistic science the
place of models in the biological and physical
sciences. The influence of graphic representation
on the development of linguistic theory is the
counterpart of the influence of models on the
development of biological and physical theory--
the double helix in biology, for instance, or the
wave model of light in physics. But what is it in
graphic representation that enables it to furnish
models for linguistic science?
      With this question, we arrive at the second
of our two perspectives on graphic representation
in linguistics. In Chapter 5, we view it from
the vantage point of the principles of graphic
design. This explains how figures can serve as
models in linguistic science: the principles of
design are by definition the principles that re-
late a figure--a graphic design--and a meaning--
the statement the design is meant to express.
They are, so to speak, the rules of correspondence
between form and meaning. Thus the two perspectives converge on a conception of graphic representation as an analogue for linguistic data. A
model is an analogue seen from the viewpoint of
the philosophy of science--the aerial view, so to
speak, looking down on it as a part of the larger
landscape of linguistic science; a graphic design
is analogue seen from the viewpoint of the principles of design--the view from inside looking
out. The relationship of analogy between figure
and datum, between design and meaning, is what

enables graphic representation to influence
linguistic theory.

Up to this point the discussion of graphic
representation in linguistics provides, not answers,
but questions: it allows us to see problems like
that of the influence of representation on theory,
but it does not tell us what to do about them--how
to undo the influence, or how to exploit it. Chapter 6 explores the possibility of new models for
linguistics, models that grow out of old ones under
the application of the principles of design. Language being the sort of thing it is, linguists
cannot hope to vindicate the models they use by
discovering actual physical structures that match
them; there will be no double helix for linguistics.
The double perspective taken here on the subject
of graphic representation in linguistics suggests,
however, that the solution to the problem of
model-building lies in more model-building.

                    Ann Harleman Stewart

Seattle, Washington
February 1975

Tree diagrams

Provenience

The tree was introduced into linguistics by August Schleicher, whose *Die deutsche Sprache*, published in 1860, contains three linguistic *Stammbäume* (Maher 1966:7). Schleicher's figure is a schematic tree:

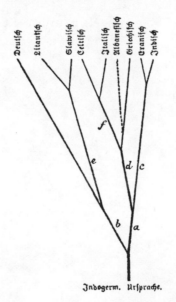

(Schleicher 1888:82)

But if Schleicher's tree is the prototype for the
tree in linguistics, what is its own prototype?
    Tree-like representation is of great age.
Sometimes stylized, sometimes realistic, trees
illustrate in medieval scholastic philosophy all
kinds of taxonomies. Thus we find a tree for the
seven liberal arts, grouping them into the Trivium
and Quadrivium; a tree of virtues and vices, embel-
lished with medallions. Not only taxonomic but
also genealogical trees appear well before the
nineteenth century--at least as early as the eight-
eenth (Barnes 1967:114). Most such early trees
look like this one:

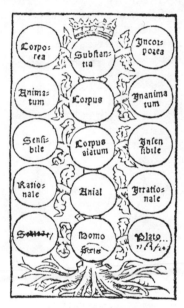

(Ong 1958:78)

    But though we can say with certainty that
tree-like representation of taxonomy and genealogy goes back well beyond Schleicher's day, we
cannot with equal certainty see in it the direct
ancestor of Schleicher's tree. For this we must
consider three possibilities: tree diagrams in

evolutionary biology; tree diagrams in human genealogy; and manuscript stemmata.
    Greenberg (1957), Hoenigswald (1963), and
Maher (1966) agree that the source of Schleicher's
tree is not the one most often supposed, Darwinian
evolutionary biology. The myth of a Darwinian linguistics originated with Schleicher himself (Hoenigswald, 6). So taken was he with the *Origin of
Species* that in 1863 he wrote *Die Darwinische Theorie und die Sprachwissenschaft*, drawing a parallel
between biological and linguistic evolution. Re-
capitulation by students of linguistics[1] magnified
the resemblance until, by a sort of *simile-huic-
ergo-propter-hoc* reasoning, Schleicher's tree
appeared to be an offshoot of Darwin's.
    This in itself of course does not disqualify
Darwin's tree as the direct ancestor of Schleicher's. A more serious objection (Maher, 7) is that
Die deutsche Sprache appeared a scant year after
the *Origin of Species*. It is unlikely, therefore,
that Schleicher knew Darwinian evolutionary theory before he formed his own theory of linguistic
evolution. And in fact, the earliest version of
Schleicher's tree appeared in 1853, well before
the *Origin of Species*:

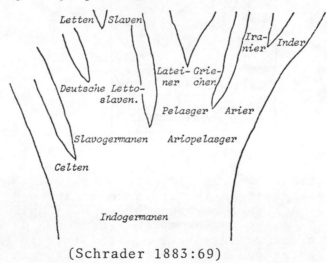

(Schrader 1883:69)

According to Schrader (1883:68), Schleicher called
this earliest version a "'sich verästelnde Baum.'"
Though not yet a "Stammbaum" (Schleicher did not
christen his figure until 1863, in *Die Darwinische
Theorie und die Sprachwissenschaft*), it conveys
the same relationships as the tree from *Die
deutsche Sprache* reproduced above. It simply replaces the letters standing for such hypothetical
linguistic unities as *Slavogermanen* (*b* in the
later version) and *Lettoslaven* (*c* in the later
version) with the names for them. Schleicher's
use of the tree diagram to express linguistic evolution thus definitely antedates Darwin's use of
it to express biological evolution.

But the *Origin of Species* was not the *début*
either of evolutionary biology or of the tree diagram. The first appearance of tree diagrams for
evolutionary biology was probably in Lamarck's
Philosophie zoologique (Simpson 1961:62). Lamarck's and Darwin's diagrams (given on the following pages) differ only slightly in form--
Lamarck's version is upside down; Darwin's is not[2]
--and not at all in meaning: Lamarck (1809:462-
464) and Darwin (1859:116-125) invest the figure
with the same meaning, that of change through time.
That Darwin's tree is not much earlier than
Schleicher's, then, does not mean that Schleicher's
tree was not drawn from evolutionary biology. A
tree that translated the meaning of change through
time--the phylogenetic meaning--had been in currency for nearly half a century by the time
Schleicher's tree appeared.

The second possible source for Schleicher's
tree, tree diagrams in human genealogy, is at
least as likely as the first. For one thing,
trees, as we have said, had been for centuries a
common shorthand for the concept of genealogy;
for another, the metaphor accompanying Schleicher's notion of linguistic evolution is that of
human genealogy. Terms like "mother-," "daugh-
ter-," and "sister-language" established this
metaphor quite early in the development of
Schleicher's theory, in *Die sprachen Europas* in

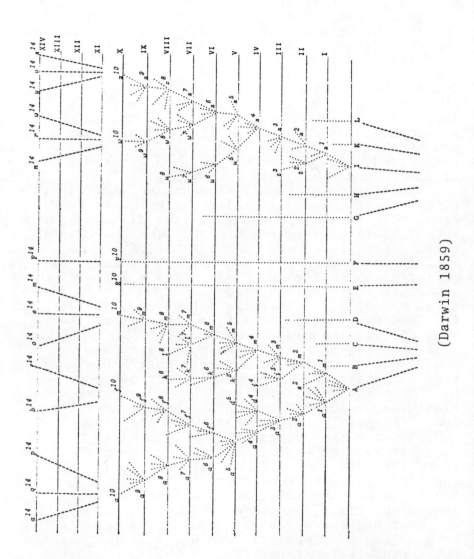

(Darwin 1859)

T A B L E A U

Servant à montrer l'origine des différens
animaux.

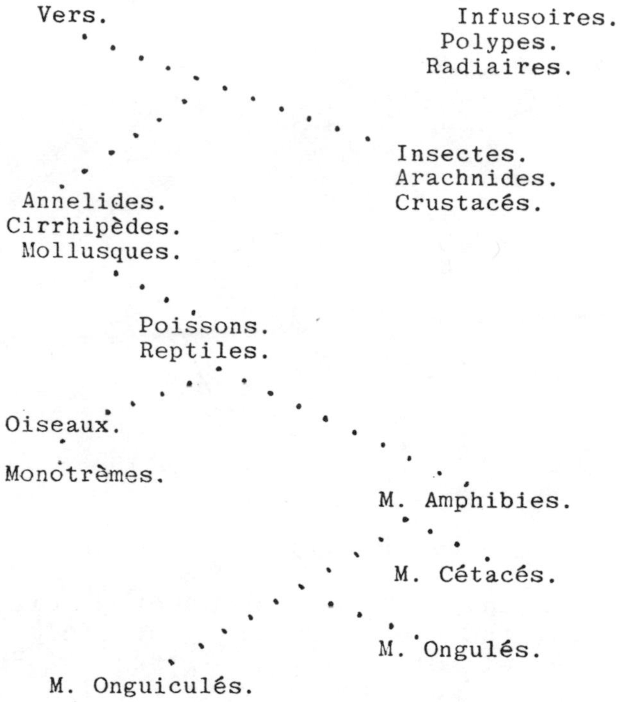

Vers.

Infusoires.
Polypes.
Radiaires.

Insectes.
Arachnides.
Crustacés.

Annelides.
Cirrhipèdes.
Mollusques.

Poissons.
Reptiles.

Oiseaux.

Monotrèmes.

M. Amphibies.

M. Cétacés.

M. Ongulés.

M. Onguiculés.

(Lamarck 1809:463)

1848 (Maher, 7). It is thus older than the figure
itself. Moreover, it had already been employed
as a metaphor for language history a century
earlier by Leibniz (Maher, 8).

It may be, however, that human genealogy
furnished the prototype for the tree diagram in
linguistics only indirectly, through the agency
of the third possible source, manuscript stemmata.
An example is the following:

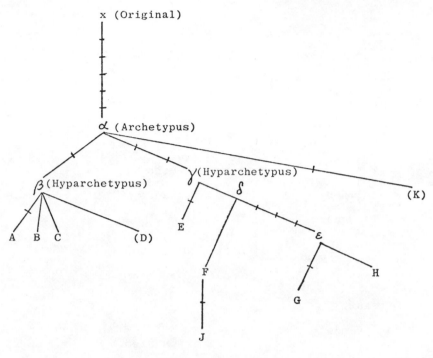

(Maas 1957:7)

In fact, both Hoenigswald (8) and Maher (8) claim
this origin for the tree, pointing out that
Schleicher, a pupil of Friedrich Ritschl at Bonn,
would have been trained in the construction of
manuscript stemmata. Hoenigswald argues that
Ritschl's theory of the construction of manuscript stemmata influenced the comparative method:
the "doctrine of the shared error" is an instance.
     Not much is to be gained from looking at the
figures themselves. Direct inspection of the trees
for historical linguistics, evolutionary biology,
and textual criticism shows the greatest resemblance between Schleicher's later version and the
one that appears in the *Origin of Species*. Both
figures are right side up; both are highly stylized (compare Schleicher's earliest version; both

mark junctures with Roman letters. A manuscript
stemma, on the other hand, is upside-down and marks
junctures with Greek letters. These differences,
nevertheless, weigh little in the scales against
the general similarity of the three figures in
form and meaning. Moreover, neither the metaphor
of evolutionary biology nor that of human genealogy can be finally discounted, for both have
influenced the course taken by the theory of
linguistic evolution since Schleicher.

Meaning

     Dangerous as it is to divorce form from con-
tent, we must do so in the case of graphic representation in linguistics. Thus we shall consider
first the form of tree diagrams: of what parts
do they consist? How are the parts put together
to form the whole? In doing so, it will of course
be impossible to avoid speaking of meaning, but
this is meaning of the most abstract sort--the
very general meaning that attaches to the figure
by virtue of the putting together of parts to
form a whole. This is not the same thing as the
meaning of a particular tree diagram--the message
with which the figure is invested in a given instance, the statement it makes about a given set
of data. That, as we shall see, is a different
matter.
     The graphic elements of a tree diagram are
the vertical and horizontal dimensions--given by
the medium itself--and nodes and branches. Vertical and horizontal have, respectively, paradigmatic and syntagmatic import: things arranged
along the vertical dimension are mutually exclusive; things arranged along the horizontal dimension are not. Thus the units on the vertical axis
are those that do not occupy the same time or
space; the units on the horizontal axis are not
subject to this restriction. If the latter are
defined negatively, this is because what they are
not is more significant than what they are, in

terms of the structure imposed on the data by the
tree diagram; units on the horizontal dimension
are defined by the fact that they do not participate in the mutual exclusivity which characterizes
units on the vertical dimension.
      We have analyzed the form of tree diagrams
into

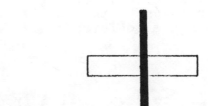

Superimposed on this is the combination of node
and branch, which gives the figure its inherent
directionality. It has a beginning and an end,
and these remain the same however the figure is
set on the page, whether it is left-to-right, top-
to-bottom, or the reverse: one starts with the
stem (the undominated node) and reads out to the
bushiest part. The tree is always divergent,
never convergent. Thus the meaning of node and
branch is former unity--former, because the unity
that exists somewhere in time or space (a node) is
explicitly said not to exist somewhere else in
time or space (the branches). So

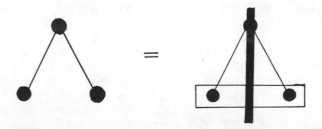

says that something splits in two under conditions
left to be stated.

Clearly, then, the basic, the most abstract, meaning of the tree leaves room for variation in meaning for given instances of the figure. Not only does the figure necessarily leave unstated the conditions under which its statement about the data holds; it is also unspecified for the domain of its application. For time and space may be variously construed. Is time, for instance, historical time, or conceptual time (as in morphological "processes")? Is space geographical space, or conceptual space (as in taxonomy)? It is true that the basic meaning of a figure to some extent circumscribes the possible meanings it can take on--to some extent sets limits to its mutability. Nevertheless, it is possible to distinguish between meanings that are a good fit for a figure and meanings that are not. The tree in linguistics bears (independent of purely graphic variation, like squared *versus* slanting branches) at least four meanings: genesis, taxonomy, componential analysis, and constituent analysis.

Genesis

Chronologically, the primary meaning of tree diagrams is, as we have seen, genetic. The genetic meaning construes the graphic elements of the figure in the following way. The vertical dimension represents time (Simpson 1961:62)--"real" time, that is, historical time, time through which change occurs. Units on the vertical axis are therefore things that succeed each other in time; they are mutually exclusive with respect to time. Conversely, units on the horizontal axis are things that occupy the same time, that are not mutually exclusive with respect to time. To put units on the same horizontal says of them nothing more than that they do not succeed each other directly. The horizontal expresses not necessarily temporal identity--simultaneity--but temporal nondistinctness. The tree can be factored into what Schleicher happily named the *Nebeneinander*

and the *Nacheinander* (Maher, 5); from a genetic tree
we can read both the succession of stages (the vertical axis: the *Nacheinander*) and the array of entities at any single stage (the horizontal axis:
the *Nebeneinander*). Schleicher put it this way:

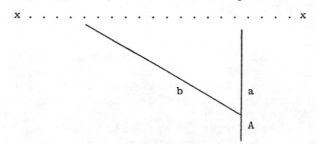

(Schleicher 1888:59)

The combination of node and branch superimposed on that of vertical and horizontal expresses
former unity; for the genetic tree, "former" is to
be taken literally, as earlier in time. Branches
then represent subsequent divergence, and the aggregate of branches from a single node constitutes
the whole set of its descendants. Branches from
a common node are more closely related to each
other than to those farther off; thus

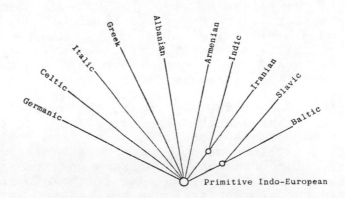

(Bloomfield 1933:312)

says (among other things) that Indic and Iranian
are more closely related to each other than to
any of the other languages, and so too Slavic and
Baltic, each pair having passed through a period
of unity.

     The meaning of the whole figure, then, is the
phylogenetic meaning: the development of a set of
related entities by means of change through time.
Besides the static meaning conveyed by the configuration of node and branches, the genetic tree
has a dynamic meaning: the figure has a starting
point and proceeds in one direction. The import
of its dynamism is "time"; but it is, in Bronowski's
words (1969:83),

>   not a forward direction in the sense of a thrust
>   towards the future, a headed arrow. What evolu-
>   tion does is to give the arrow of time a barb
>   which stops it from running backward.

This dynamism is often the focus of modified versions of the genetic tree--what might be called
"details" from the whole figure--like those of
Bloomfield:

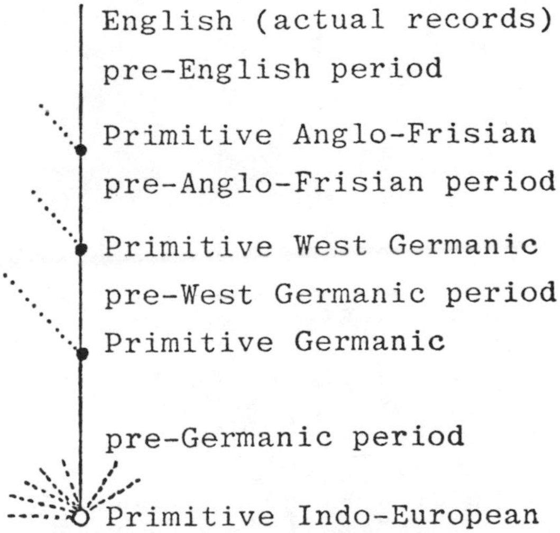

English (actual records)

pre-English period

Primitive Anglo-Frisian

pre-Anglo-Frisian period

Primitive West Germanic

pre-West Germanic period

Primitive Germanic

pre-Germanic period

Primitive Indo-European

(Bloomfield 1933:312)

and Trager and Smith:

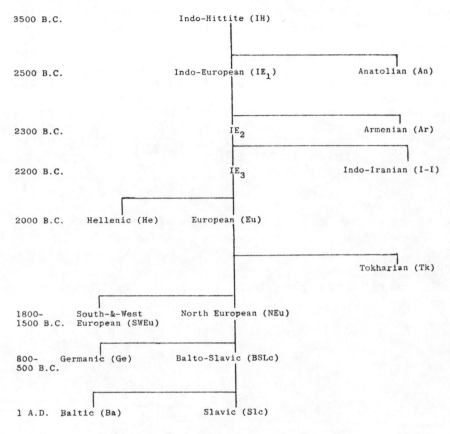

(Trager and Smith 1950:64)

They are offshoot diagrams: at any given stage,
only one entity occurs. Nowhere is there a set of
two or more entities occupying the same horizontal,
so that there is nothing that might properly be
called the *Nebeneinander*. They focus on the *Nacheinander*--Bloomfield's on the successive stages in
the development of a single language out of Indo-
European, Trager and Smith's on the successive reduction of Indo-European as the daughter languages

split off from it. If such offshoot diagrams have
a destination--in Bloomfield's figure, English; in
Trager and Smith's, Slavic--it is something in the
present or something already past, never something
in the future. It is in this sense that Bronowski's
barbed arrow is appropriate.

Taxonomy

     Related to the genetic meaning of tree dia-
grams is the taxonomic meaning. Because the graphic elements of the tree are construed differently
for the two meanings, however, they are only related, not identical. The vertical dimension in a
taxonomic tree diagram signifies not time, but
space: points along the vertical axis represent
not stages in the development of a language family out of a single parent language, but stages
in the successive partitioning of a set. Units
on the vertical axis are things that succeed each
other in space--the conceptual space furnished by
the set that is being partitioned--just as in a
genetic tree diagram units on the vertical axis
are things that succeed each other in time. They
are in paradigmatic relation to each other, mutually exclusive with respect to space. Conversely,
units on the horizontal axis are things that occupy the same space, that are not mutually exclusive with respect to space, that are in a syntagmatic relation. An example is Pike's taxonomy of
continuants:

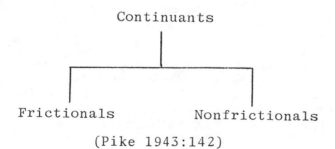

(Pike 1943:142)

Frictionals and Nonfrictionals, a syntagmatic pair,
share the same space--a space from which they have
dislodged Continuants, so that the pair Friction-
als/Nonfrictionals is in a paradigmatic relation
with Continuants.

The graphic elements of node and branch set
the boundaries of the relations among units. As
in a genetic tree, branches from a common node are
more closely related to each other than to those
farther off; in a taxonomic tree this is proximity
not in time but in space, and branches from a
common node define subsets. In the example given
above, for instance, Frictionals and Nonfrictionals are proper subsets of the set of Continuants,
and together they exhaust the set.

We can restate our analysis of the taxonomic
tree in terms of set theory. The set-theoretic
definition of a taxonomy (Gregg 1954:47-51) is:

1.   It is a hierarchy
2.   It is a one-many relation
3.   It has a "unique beginner"
4.   No unit is equal to that dominating it
5.   No two levels have members in common
6.   It is an asymmetrical relation
7.   It is an irreflexive relation
8.   It is an intransitive relation
9.   For any two members of its field, either
     y includes x, or x includes y, or they
     are mutually exclusive
10. "The converse of a taxonomic system is
     never a taxonomic system"

Perhaps it will be useful to translate these theo-
rems back into graphic terms. The first four the-
orems are implicit in our interpretation of the
combination of node and branch. The tree figure
is hierarchical by virtue of branching, which gives
it a beginning and an end. A one-many relationship
is what branching from a single node is. By definition the tree figure has a unique beginner--that
is, it starts from a single node and is divergent,
not convergent. No unit is equal to that dominating it, because a node, if it branches at all,

must necessarily give way to two or more nodes.
The fifth, sixth, seventh, eighth, and tenth theo-
rems are implicit in our interpretation of the
vertical dimension in the tree. Because units
succeed each other along the vertical dimension,
no two points on it can have members in common;
nor can succession, by definition, be either symmetrical (two units each succeeding the other) or
reflexive (a unit succeeding itself). Transitiv-
ity is not ruled out by definition; but if two
units separated by a third are seen, in accord
with the notion of hierarchy, as linked only
through that third intervening unit, then transi-
tivity too is impossible. And, of course, the
converse of a taxonomic system cannot be a taxonomic system, for the tree proceeds in one direction and cannot be read backwards.

It is the ninth theorem, which states the
admissible relations among units on the horizontal dimension, that is troublesome for the taxonomic tree in linguistics. We can interpret this
theorem, following Kay (1970), in terms of Venn
diagrams; for the admissible relations between
taxa:

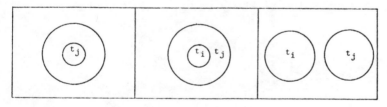

(Kay 1970:8)

for the prohibited relation:

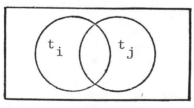

(Kay 1970:9)

Taxa--whether they are nodes or terminal elements--
can be related in one of two ways. Either they
participate in the paradigmatic relation, which we
have defined as the vertical dimension, so that for
any two units one is a proper subset of the other
(the first two Venn diagrams above); or they participate in the syntagmatic relation, which we have
defined as the horizontal dimension, so that any
two units are wholly separate (the third Venn diagram). What they may not do is participate at
once in both the paradigmatic relation and the syntagmatic relation. They may not constitute intersecting classes.
      What about the taxonomic tree in linguistics?
Here the definition of admissible relations among
taxa becomes a problem. Compare Bloomfield's (1933:
205) classification of nouns in English,

    I.   Names (proper nouns)
   II.   Common nouns
    A.   Bounded nouns
    B.   Unbounded nouns
    1.   Mass nouns
    2.   Abstract nouns

with Chomsky's "subcategorization" of them:

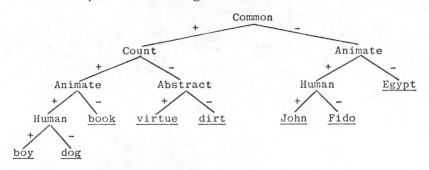

(Chomsky 1965:83)

Taxonomic trees in linguistics usually fail the
requirement that classes not overlap. Because
the feature [± Animate] appears at more than one
node, Chomsky's subcategorization shows four
intersecting taxa:

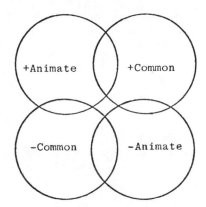

That is, some common nouns denote animate objects,
and some do not; some proper nouns denote animate
objects, and some do not. Though this is clearly
an accurate statement, it is not a proper taxonomy.
Bloomfield's classification is. It yields a taxonomic tree in which no feature appears at more
than one node and in which, therefore, no classes
overlap:

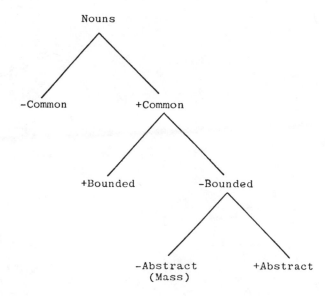

Pike proposes, as an alternative to the taxonomy of continuants we have looked at, a tree that
fails the same requirement as Chomsky's subcategorization of nouns:

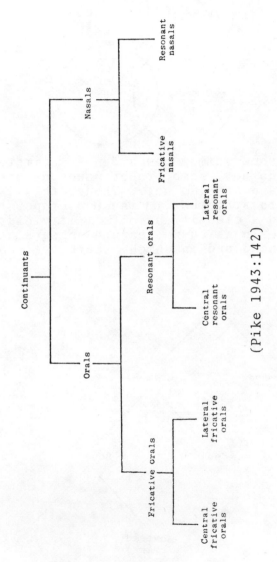

(Pike 1943:142)

He thereupon presents a dendrogram that faces in
two directions at once:

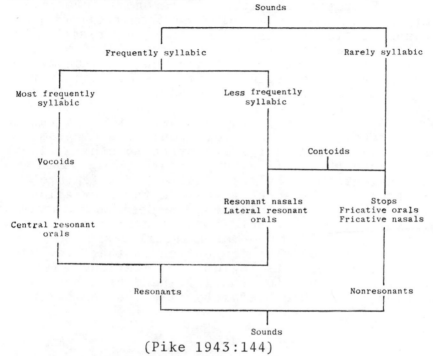

(Pike 1943:144)

By representing his classification by a sort of
Rorschach tree, Pike avoids putting features at
more than one node; but overlapping classes are
to be inferred--for instance,

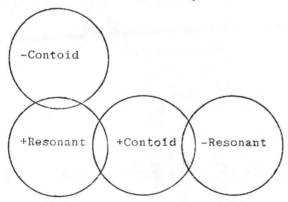

It seems, then, that linguists do not follow
a set theoretic definition of taxonomic classification. This is to be inferred from their graphic
representation. Pike's *Phonetics*, for example, is
probably the most explicitly taxonomic of modern
linguistic treatments; yet the meager taxonomy we
looked at in the beginning of this section is the
only diagram we have considered from it that is a
proper taxonomy. Nida (1964:74) explicitly allows
overlapping classes. Though there exists a taxonomic meaning for the tree, then, tree diagrams
presented as taxonomies are often something else.
     Hence the difficulty presented, for transfor-
mational grammar, by tree diagrams for feature
hierarchies: because linguistic taxonomy allows
overlapping feature-classes, the desired relations
of implication that hold among features are not,
as is often held, to be automatically and unambiguously inferred. The contention is that reading
up the tree reflects logical implication. Yet
this is true only for the left-hand branches in
a semantic feature hierarchy like the one below:

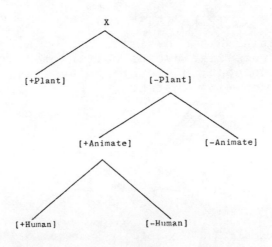

(Bever and Rosenbaum 1970:6)

Thus [+Human] implies [+Animate] implies [-Plant];
but [-Human] does not necessarily imply [+Animate],
nor does [-Animate] necessarily imply [-Plant].
What has gone wrong here is that these features
name what are in reality, logically and semanti-
cally, overlapping classes.[3] The class named by
[-Animate], for example, embraces not only some
of the members of the class [-Plant], but also all
of the members of the class [+Plant] and all of
the members of the class [-Human]. Similarly, the
class named by [-Human] embraces not only some of
the members of the class [+Animate] but also all
of the members of the class [-Animate] and all of
the members of the class [+Plant].

Componential analysis

     Trees expressing componential analysis look
in every way like their fellows; but they do not
mean the same thing. Like Chomsky's subcategorization of English nouns, the lexical entry for
bachelor applies features ([±Male] and [±Young])
at more than one node (see following page). It
is a simple matter to make the figure conform to
the criteria for taxonomy by reordering the
features:

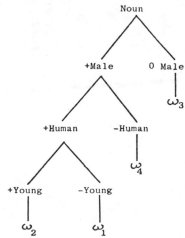

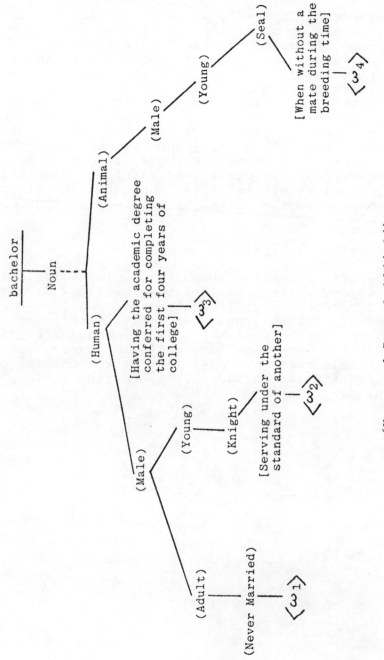

(Katz and Postal 1964:14)

To do so solves nothing, however, because the
meaning of lexical entries is not taxonomy.
Lexical entry and taxonomy are not synonymous.
     The meaning of trees expressing componential
analysis is in a sense the opposite of taxonomy.
These trees are what are called "keys" in biology
and anthropology (Conklin, 1964 and personal
communication). A key sets out a componential
analysis of the units that are its terminal
elements, an analysis in which the components
are distinctive features. This is a schematic
version of a key:

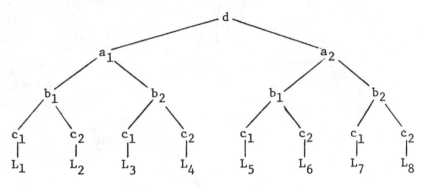

(Simpson 1961:52)

Here the analysis of units L_1 - L_8 is given in
terms of the distinctive features $a_{1,2}$, $b_{1,2}$,
and $c_{1,2}$--equivalent to [±a], [±b], [±c]. The
element L_1 is analyzed as [a_1, b_1, c_1], the
element L_2 as [a_1, b_1, c_2], and so on. The
beginner, *d*, is a dummy feature; it is not
distinctive within the analysis, but simply
defines the whole set L_1 - L_8. The lexical entry
tree for *bachelor* is actually a telescoped
version of the following key:

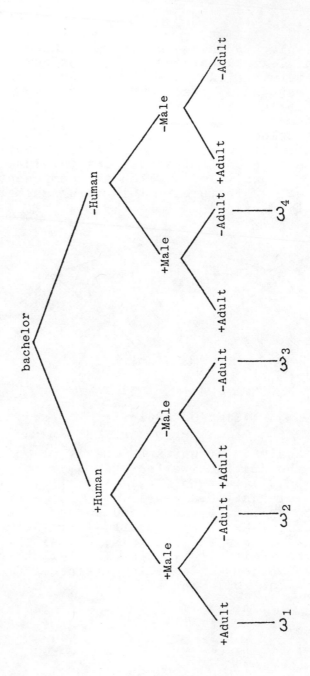

Chomsky's subcategorization of nouns--because it
violates the set-theoretic restriction on overlapping classes--is also a telescoped version of
a key:

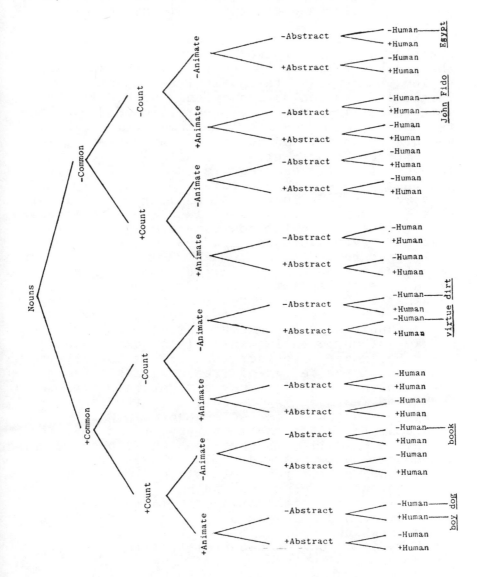

The sequence of features along the vertical is the
same for the original diagrams as for the full
keys, and so is the sequence of terminal elements
along the horizontal. The original diagrams are
telescoped in comparison with the full keys in the
sense that elements along both dimensions are
omitted.

We can call the diagrams both of Katz and
Postal and of Chomsky keys, because both construe
the graphic elements of the tree in the same way
as keys. Keys, like taxonomic trees, construe the
vertical dimension as conceptual space, within
which a set is successively partitioned; keys, like
taxonomic trees, construe the combination of node
and branch as set and subsets. But whereas taxonomic trees do not--or should not--allow overlapping classes, keys require them. A full key
has them on every row; a telescoped key like the
ones we have been looking at usually has at least
some. Because of this, keys lack the directionality of genetic and taxonomic tree diagrams. In a
full key, every terminal element is specified for
every feature. Whether we read from top to bottom
or bottom to top makes no difference. The analysis
of each terminal element comes out the same: to
say that $L_1 = a_1 + b_1 + c_1$ is the same as saying
that $a_1 + b_1 + c_1 = L_1$. It is only the figure,
as a graphic design, that has directionality; the
meaning of componential analysis as expressed in
a key has none. The fact that directionality is
inherent in the design of tree diagrams lets the
key incorporate a hierarchy of features. The sequence of features in the lexical entry for *bachelor*, for instance, is the sequence in which,
according to this semantic theory, these features
are hierarchically arranged; but as Simpson (1961:
55) points out, this order "is derived from the
corresponding hierarchic classification and is
not inherent in the key as such."

So it is that reordering the features on the
tree for *bachelor* is useless. For one thing, the
order in which features occur is fixed; for
another, it is only accidental that the tree for

bachelor converts to a true taxonomy. The subcategorization of English nouns that we looked at
earlier, having overlapping classes, does not.
And it is unimaginable for, say, Halle's key for
the sounds of Russian:

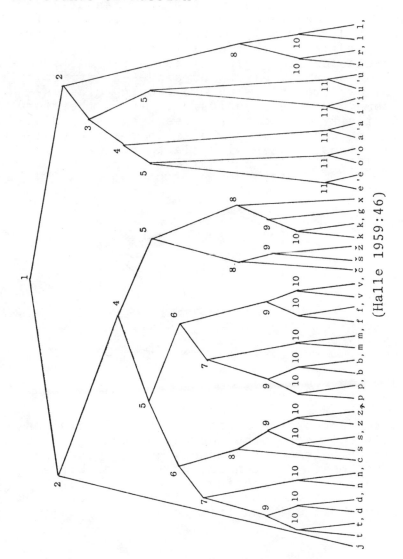

(Halle 1959:46)

Yet the problem for linguistics is even more
complicated than this: beyond the confusion that
results from employing the same diagram to represent the two different meanings of taxonomy and
componential analysis, there is the confusion
that results from employing the same features for
the names of both taxa and components. The difficulty of drawing all and only the proper inferences regarding implicational relations among
feature-classes from such a tree as the one from
Bever and Rosenbaum discussed above--a difficulty
that follows from allowing overlapping classes--
is compounded by this confusion. It is therefore
only partially solved by representing the classification as what it properly is in componential-
analysis terms, a key--with blank spots where
inadmissible feature-combinations occur:

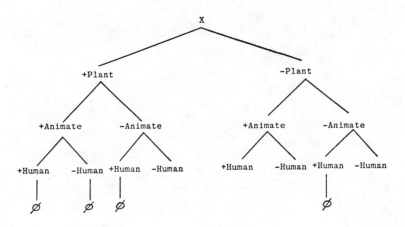

Such a representation is only a partial solution
precisely because of the confusion, both graphic
and terminological, of taxonomy and componential
analysis: what is intended, what is in fact
desired here, is a blending of the two. For
linguistics, it must be possible to read off from
such a tree not only an artificial, analysis-

imposed classification--a taxonomy--that ignores
the practical reality of overlapping classes, but
also simultaneously an accurate statement of the
implicational relations that hold among the criteria for classification--the components--for any
given single instance of real analysis.[4] We shall
reserve a more detailed discussion of this problem
for a later consideration of the possibility of
representing graphically such a double meaning.

Constituent analysis

        This might more properly be called immediate
constituent analysis (IC analysis). An example
is the following, a tree for IC analysis at the
level of the sentence:

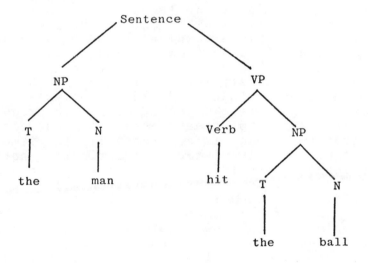

(Chomsky 1957:27)

Analysis of the graphic elements in each of the
other three kinds of tree diagrams showed their
meanings to be related. Taxonomy results from,
and often recapitulates, phylogeny; componential
analysis implies a prior taxonomy (that is, a
hierarchical classification of the features
employed). The first three meanings are thus
related in a sort of chain. Constituent analysis,
however, stands apart from this chain. It has in
common with the others only the basic meaning of
the tree design itself.
     The vertical dimension expresses succession;
not succession in time or space, but simply
succession. In the example above, NP, for instance, gives way to T and N; VP gives way to Verb
and NP; and so on. The relation expressed by the
combination of node and branch is thus to be
read, not "becomes" (as in a genetic tree), nor
"includes" (as in a taxonomic tree), nor "is di-
vided into" (as in a key), but simply "may be
replaced by." This is the technique of immediate
constituent analysis itself: it is the process
of substitution. (The reading of "becomes" that
is attributed to the vertical dimension of the
tree in generative grammar is a misreading. It
results from misconstruing the meaning of the tree
as something other than constituent analysis--
usually as "generative process" or speech production. The meaning of tree diagrams of sentences
in generative grammar is substantially the same
as in structural linguistics: description, not
production [Chomsky 1965:9], the description of
a sentence in terms of its constituents.) The
horizontal dimension of trees for constituent
analysis expresses syntagmatic relatedness; in
the example above, T and N form one syntagm, Verb
and NP another, and so on. Units in the same row
are not mutually exclusive, not substitutable one
for another. In IC trees, then, the significance
attributed to the vertical and horizontal dimensions adds nothing to the expression of hierarchy
already conveyed by the combination of node and
branch.

Node and branch also express constituent
function (Chomsky 1965:68-74). The difference
between Subject and Object, for instance is
conveyed by

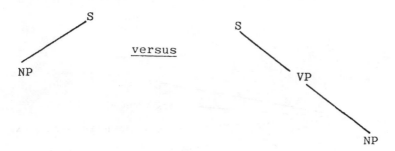

The figure entails this difference: it is
automatic.
    There is a further difference between IC
trees and other kinds, and that is the fact that
no units need appear at the nodes of the tree.

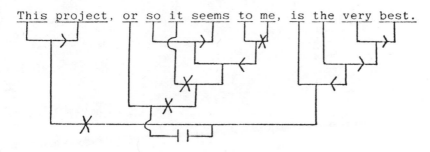

(Nida 1966:21)

Here, just as in the first example, the meaning
is immediate constituent analysis. Its expression
is unhampered by the lack of category symbols like
NP, VP, and so on; which terminal units are constituents of which constructions at which level
is quite clear.

The four meanings of tree diagrams, then, are
genesis, taxonomy, componential analysis, and
constituent analysis. Even the modest collection
of diagrams we have accumulated here shows the
existence of homonymy for graphic representation
in linguistics:

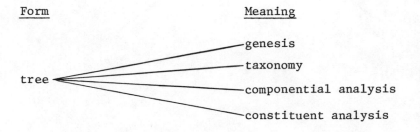

Form   Meaning

tree ┬ genesis
     ├ taxonomy
     ├ componential analysis
     └ constituent analysis

Matrix diagrams

Provenience

    The arrangement of things in a table--a ma-
trix arrangement--appears to be as old as written
records; lists or inventories arranged in tables
figure prominently among the Linear B tablets, for
example. In linguistics, the matrix is perhaps
as old as Indian grammatical theory. The characters of the *devanāgarī* alphabet[5] are usually given
in a matrix arrangement. The arrangement of the
symbols for stops and nasals given by Whitney as

		surd	surd asp.	sonant	son. asp.	nasal
	guttural	¹⁷ क k	¹⁸ ख kh	¹⁹ ग g	²⁰ घ gh	²¹ ङ ñ
	palatal	²² च c	²³ छ ch	²⁴ ज j	²⁵ झ jh	²⁶ ञ ñ
Mutes	lingual	²⁷ ट ṭ	²⁸ ठ ṭh	²⁹ ड ḍ	³⁰ ढ ḍh	³¹ ण ṇ
	dental	³² त t	³³ थ th	³⁴ द d	³⁵ ध dh	³⁶ न n
	labial	³⁷ प p	³⁸ फ ph	³⁹ ब b	⁴⁰ भ bh	⁴¹ म m

       (Whitney 1889:2)

and by Allen as

Consonants			Labial	Dental	Retroflex	Palatal	Velar	'Glottal'
Stops	Voiceless	Unaspirated	p̲ / p	t̲ / t	ṭ̲ / ṭ	c̲ / c	k̲ / k	
		Aspirated	p̲h / ph	t̲h / th	ṭ̲h / ṭh	c̲h / ch	k̲h / kh	
	Voiced	Unaspirated	b̲ / b	d̲ / d	ḍ̲ / ḍ	j̲ / j	g̲ / g	
		Aspirated	b̲h / bh	d̲h / dh	ḍ̲h / ḍh	j̲h / jh	g̲h / gh	
Nasals			m̲ / m	n̲ / n	ṇ̲ / ṇ	ñ̲ / ñ	ṅ̲ / ṅ	

(Allen 1953:20)

expresses a classification of the sounds based on their analysis according to articulatory features. Neither Whitney nor Allen says whether or not the

matrix arrangement occurs in the ancient works;
but the sequence (given by the numbers beside the
characters in Whitney's figure) of the letters is
that of the *varṇa-samāmnāya*. Cardona points out
(personal communication) that, in any case, "we
cannot literally speak of a written chart: such
lists were always recited only."
      We are on firmer ground, then, with the analysis
presented by the figure than with the figure itself.
Sounds with the same place of articulation are a
varga, which Allen translates "class," and Whitney,
"series." Such subgroups were useful for general-
izations: Bloomfield (1929:271) cites Pāṇini's
practice of referring to a group of letters by the
first letter of the group and the "silent letter"
following it in the *samāmnāya* sequence. Sounds
with the same manner of articulation are indicated
by numbering alike corresponding members of the
five classes (Allen, 47). Thus the two dimensions
of the matrix are defined just as they are for
modern articulatory phonetics. For instance, Whitney's first column, which is the same as Allen's
first row, is the set of voiceless unaspirated
stops /k c t t p/--a set of sounds sharing the
same manner of articulation; in a modern articulatory matrix, they would constitute a single row,
/p t t k k/. Whitney's first row, which is the
same as Allen's first column, is the set of velars
/k k^h g g^h ŋ/--a set of sounds sharing the same
place of articulation; in a modern articulatory
matrix, they would constitute a single column. In
the matrix derived from the *varṇa-samāmnāya*, then,
rows and columns are sets of sound alike in place
or manner, sets of sounds sharing particular features: for the set /k c t t p/, these features
are [-Voice], [-Tense], and [-Continuant]. The
varṇa-samāmnāya of the Hindu grammarians is in
fact a componential analysis. In Prague School
terms, the set of twenty-five consonants may be
factored into series (Whitney's column; Allen's
row) and order (Whitney's row; Allen's column).
The set of voiceless stops /k c t t p/ is a series;
the set of velars /k k^h g g^h ŋ/ is an order.

Until the second half of the nineteenth
century, matrix diagrams are rare. Exceptions
are in works so little known that their authors
are among those dubbed by Abercrombie (1948)
"forgotten phoneticians." Francis Lodwick,
in his "Essay Towards an Universal Alphabet"
of 1648, is one of these:

The Univerſall Alphabet .

The Table of Conſonants						
1	2	3	4	5	6	7
1 ꟾ b	ꟾ d	ꟾ J	Ꮞ g	ꟾ =	ꟾ =	P ſ
2 ꟾ P	ꟾ t	ꟾ ch	Ꮞ k	ꟾ =	ꟾ =	
3 ꟾ m	ꟾ n	ꟾ gñ	Ꮞ n͡g	ꟾ =	ꟾ =	
4 ꟾ =	ꟾ dh	ꟾ J	Ꮞ g	ꟾ v	ꟾ z	B ſh
5 ꟾ =	ꟾ th	ꟾ sh	Ꮞ ch	ꟾ f	ꟾ s	
6	ꟾ ñ					

8	9	10	11	12		
ꟾ k	ꟾ y	ꟾ r	ꟾ w	ꟾ א		

(Abercrombie 1948:9)

Here as elsewhere the matrix implies a
componential analysis.
    In the late nineteenth and early twentieth
centuries, with the interest in analphabetic
notation--which, by definition, carries with it
a componential analysis--that appears to have
begun with Alexander Melville Bell's *Visible
Speech*, the matrix gained wider currency. It
serves in Bell's work as the ground on which
are displayed the analphabetic characters:

	CONSONANTS.				Key Words.			VOWELS.*				Key Words.		
Back.	Front.	Point.	Lip.					Back.	Mixed.	Front.				
										ſ		see ear		
	↻	ω			yes	race		]		[	up urh	say		
	Ω	ʊ	ɔ		so	show	why			ʇ		ell		
	Ω	ʊ	ϑ		ooze	rouge	we	]*	ʇ˦	ſ	-tion -tious -er	the -es	ill	
			ʒ				few	]	ʇ	ɛ	ask	a -al -ance	air -ed -ment	
		ω	ϑ			lay	view	ʇ	ɪ	ʇ	ah arm	err	an	
	Ω				thin			ʇ			pool			
	Ω				then			ʇ			go			
ɑ		ʊ	ɒ	key		tea	pea	ʇ			law			
ɑ		ʊ	ϑ	gay		day	bay	ʇ	ɪ*		poor good	-ure -ful		
								ʇ	ʇ˧		ore	-ory		
ɑ		ʊ	ϑ	sing		sin	him	ʇ	ɪ*		on or	-or -ward		

(Bell 1867:110)

This Bell labels (1867:110) "table of English
elements, showing their position in the universal
alphabet." The matrix arrangement interprets the
notation: it is taken for granted that placing
the symbols on the ground provided by the matrix--
showing their positions in a "universal," or at
any rate a fuller, inventory of sounds--somehow
translates a far from accessible notation. Henry
Sweet employs the matrix in a like manner for his
"'Organic' (revised Visible Speech) notation"
(1890:vii):

℩		⦵	ω	∪,ᴡ	s, ʂ	ʐ,ɛ		ᴐ,ɘ	>,⪢
—					ω				
	ɑ,ɘ				ᴑ,ᴡ		ᴆ,ɘ		
—	⅃				ꞁ		ꟻ		

206. The Broad Romic equivalents are:

b	= ᴆ	*as in*	bee.
d	= ᴡ	„	day.
ð (dh)	= ᴜ	„	then.
f	= ⊃	„	fall.
g	= ᴇ	„	go.
h	= ℩	„	house.
j	= ⦵	„	you.
k	= ɑ	„	come.
l	= ω	„	look.
m	= ꟻ	„	man.
n	= ꞁ	„	no.
ŋ	= ⅃	„	sing.
p	= ᴆ	„	pay.
r	= ω	„	red.
s	= s	„	say.
ʃ (sh)	= ɛ	„	ship.
t	= ᴑ	„	ten.
þ (th)	= ᴜ	„	thin.

(Sweet 1890:77)

The reader's impulse to leaf through the book
until he comes upon just such a presentation
argues that it renders the system intelligible--
in outline if not in detail--that it is a map the
reader can carry with him into the analphabetic
wilderness.[6]

How can a figure seldom met explain symbols
even less familiar? We can resolve this by back-
tracking a little to examine the concept of
phonological space. Moulton (1962:24-25) traces
it back as far as Grimm's *Deutsche Grammatik*, and

finds it implicit in subsequent works like Hermann
Paul's *Prinzipien der Sprachgeschichte* (1880) and
Karl Luick's *Untersuchungen zur Lautgeschichte*
(1896). The notion of phonological space in the
linguistics of the nineteenth century accounts for
the appearance, in the works of Bell and Sweet, of
the matrix. Phrases like those Moulton finds in
Grimm ("'occupy a position,'" "'move from a position,'" "'fill a gap'") and in Paul ("'directions'
in which phonemes 'move'"), metaphoric or not,
presuppose a matrix arrangement of sounds. This
matrix arrangement must have underlain the notion
of phonological space, if not on paper then at
least in the minds of its proponents.

Meaning

     The matrix expresses a single meaning, compo-
nential analysis. It does not, like the tree,
comprise several meanings; but it does comprise
two graphic variants whose difference lies in how
the data are displayed on the figure. We shall
leave them for the moment, to consider the matrix
as a design.
     The design of the matrix rests on three
graphic elements: rows, columns, and cells. All
have their meaning by virtue of contrast. Contrast, indeed, is what makes the figure. By virtue
of the contrast between the two dimensions, rows
and columns have their meaning: a row or column
incorporates the meaning of the dimension along
which it lies and the meaning of the dimension on
which it is a locus. Thus, in Whitney's figure,
the first row means "all and only the velar consonants": "all" because it lies along the horizontal dimension, "only" because it is a locus on the
vertical. Similarly, the first column means "all
and only the voiceless unaspirated consonants":
"all" because it lies along the vertical dimension,
"only" because it is a locus on the horizontal. A
cell is simultaneously a locus on both dimensions;

its meaning is thus the product of the meanings
ascribed to the two dimensions. It is because of
this that Bell's figure can translate his notation.
Bell defines each symbol as its position in the
universal alphabet--the universal alphabet being
the matrix arrangement of all speech sounds, and
position being meant literally, as the location
of a particular sound in this arrangement. We
know by its location that Ꝑ , for example, is to
be translated [p]--because it is plotted on the
row labelled (by means of the key word *key*) "voiceless," and the column labelled "lip":

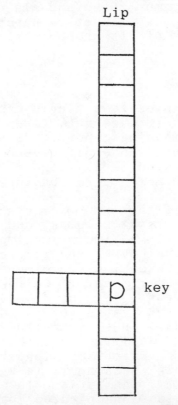

Conversely, the meanings assigned to the two
dimensions may be inferred if the value of the
sound in any cell is known. Labels are then

unnecessary: this is how we are able to read Lodwick's diagram of the "universal alphabet." And
because every cell is the intersection of the two
dimensions, it is possible to determine what would
be in an empty cell, were it filled; indeed, not
only possible, but inescapable. The empty cells
in this diagram from Trubetzkoy, for instance,

p	t	k	ʕ
——	t^h	k^h	
——	s	x	h
m	n	——	——

+ r

(Trubetzkoy 1939:153)

are clearly /p^h ɸ ŋ ŋ̣/.
     The matrix figure, as we have seen, has no
top or bottom, left or right. Its meaning is the
same, whether a given matrix is

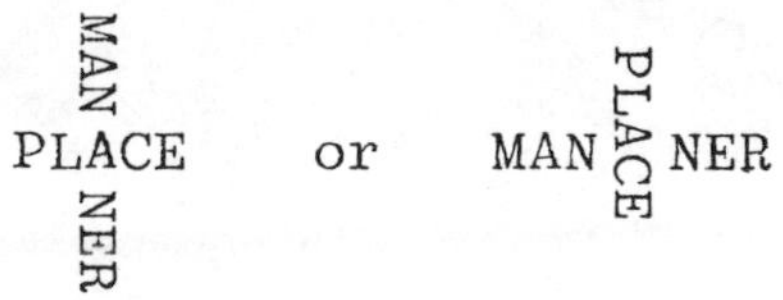

          MAN   PLACE
          PLACE   or   MAN   NER
          NER

The matrix, unlike the tree, has no directionality.
It is for this reason that the meaning of empty
cells can be inferred--or rather, both the lack
of directionality and the possibility of inferring
the meaning of empty cells are the result of a
characteristic of the design which we shall take
up later. For the time being, note that in a
matrix diagram, as on a map, every point in space

is *a priori* defined, and labels need not be
included. The latitudes and longitudes, so to
speak, are given; and place names, though handy,
are not necessary. We may think of matrix diagrams as maps of phonological space.

Componential analysis in a matrix

        Though the meaning of matrix diagrams is
always componential analysis, there are two ways
in which they are used to express this meaning.
The first we shall call the matrix; the second,
the grid. All of the examples we have looked at
so far are of the first sort. For its use in
modern articulatory phonetics, the matrix has
a key something like this:

		Labial		Alveolar	Alveo-palatal	Velar
		Bilabial	Labio-dental			
Stop	Voiceless					
	Voiced					
Nasal						
Lateral						
Flap						
Trill						
Frica-ative	Voiceless					
	Voiced					

        (Pike 1947:195 [phonetic symbols omitted])

However, this sort of diagram appears for articulatory phonetics as early as Sievers's work (see
following page). The notion of componential
analysis is implicit in such a matrix, just as
the technique of componential analysis is implicit
in articulatory phonetics.
        Componential analysis is explicit in the use
of matrix diagrams in the work of Trubetzkoy.
Nearly all of the figures in the *Grundzüge* are
matrix diagrams. They show not only the inventory
of phonemes but also their pattern--the system of

| | | Lippenlaute | | Zungengaumenlaute | | | | | | | | Faucallaute | Laryngall. |
| | | Labiale | Labiodentale | Coronale | | | Supradentale | | Dorsale | | Laterale | | |
				Cerebrale	Interdentale	Postdentale	Coronal-alveolare	Dorsal-alveolare	Palatale	Gutturale	Cerebral— / palatal / (guttural?)		
Momentane Laute / Geräuschlaute	Explosivlaute stimmlos	$p, \breve{b}$	$(p, \breve{b})$	$\underset{.}{t}, \underset{.}{\breve{d}}$	$t^1, \breve{d}^1$	$t^2, \breve{d}^2$	$t^3, \breve{d}^3$	$t^4, \breve{d}^4$	$c^1, c^2; \breve{j}^1, \breve{j}^2$	$k^1, k^2; \breve{g}^1, \breve{g}^2$	$t[l]$ etc.	$p[m], t[n]$ etc.	' (S.138 f.)
	Explosivlaute stimmhaft	$\breve{b}$	$(\breve{b})$	$\underset{.}{\breve{d}}$	d^1	d^2	d^3	d^4	$\breve{j}^1, \breve{j}^2$	g^1, g^2	$[dl]$ etc.	$\breve{b}[m], \breve{d}[n]$ etc.	—
Dauerlaute / Geräuschlaute	Spiranten stimmlos	$\breve{w}$	f	$\underset{.}{s}, \underset{.}{\check{s}}$	$\theta^1, s^1(?)$	$\theta^2; s^2$	$s^3, \check{s}^1$	$s^4, \check{s}^2$	$\varsigma, \check{\delta}^1; \chi^1, \chi^2$	$\chi^1, \chi^2; x^1, x^2$	stimmlose spir. l	[Schnarchen, S.51]	' (S.140) Flüstergeräusch (S.27) (S.27 f.)
	Spiranten stimmhaft	w	v	$\underset{.}{z}, \underset{.}{\check{z}}$	$\check{\delta}^1, z^1(?)$	$\check{\theta}^2; z^2$	$z^3, \check{z}^1$	$z^4, \check{z}^2$	$\acute{z}, \check{z}^1; \acute{j}^1, \acute{j}^2$	$\acute{\jmath}^1, \acute{\jmath}^2; \check{z}^1, \check{z}^2$	stimmhafte sp. l	—	—
Dauerlaute / Sonorlaute	Nasale	m	(m)	$\underset{.}{\check{n}}$	n^1	n^2	n^3	n^4	$\tilde{n}^1, \tilde{n}^2$	η^1, η^2	(alle l-Laute)		
	l-Laute									$(l?)$			
	l-Laute	(r)	—	$\underset{.}{\check{l}}$	—	$(r?)$	l^3	l^4	l'^1, l'^2	$(l?)$	—		
	r-Laute			$\underset{.}{r}$			r^1, r^2	r^4		r^3		[bisweilen Schnarch.]	ɼ

(Sievers 1881:106)

correlations in which they stand. Empty cells, as well, give information about pattern. The absence of /pʰ ɸ ŋ ɲ/ in Trubetzkoy's diagram, for instance, signifies the absence of the contrasts [±Continuant] and [±Nasal] in part of the system--a statement about pattern. Here the boundary of the figure is also exploited. The position of /r/ "ausserhalb des Korrelationsystems" (Trubetzkoy 1939: 153) is represented by putting it precisely there. Outside the boundary is outside the pattern.

There are, of course, differences among matrix diagrams. First, particular matrices differ in domain. The area mapped by one matrix may be larger or smaller or altogether different from that mapped by another. A diagram like Pike's (on page 48) for the sounds of a particular language does not map the same area as the matrix arrangement for the International Phonetic Alphabet (at right), the domain of which is all speech sounds. Secondly, particular matrices differ in ostensible

	Bi-labial	Labio-dental	Dental and Alveolar	Retroflex	Palato-alveolar	Alveolo-palatal	Palatal	Velar	Uvular	Pharyngal	Glottal
Plosive	p b		t d	ʈ ɖ			c ɟ	k g	q ɢ		ʔ
Nasal	m	ɱ	n	ɳ			ɲ	ŋ	ɴ		
Lateral Fricative			ɬ ɮ								
Lateral Non-fricative			l	ɭ		ʎ					
Rolled			r						ʀ		
Flapped			ɾ	ɽ			ɟ		ʀ		
Fricative	ɸ β	f v	θ ð s z	ʂ ʐ	ʃ ʒ		ç ʝ	x ɣ	χ ʁ	ħ ʕ	h ɦ
Frictionless Continuants and Semi-vowels	w ɥ	ʋ	ɹ				j (ɥ)	(w)	ʁ		

CONSONANTS

(Pike 1947:232)

purpose. The matrix of Bell and Sweet is a glos-
sary; that of the IPA, an inventory; that of
Trubetzkoy, an explicit representation of system
or pattern. In the first sort, the sounds are
ostensibly of no account; in the second sort, the
sounds are simply themselves; in the third sort,
the sounds are more than themselves, for a matrix
representation of a system of correlations breaks
down the sounds into their components and at the
same time builds out of them the structure of a
sound system.
     Finally, particular matrices differ in design:
modification of the matrix figure may follow upon
the purpose for which it is used. For instance,
the configuration can be tailored to the pattern
of the sound system represented--as in another
figure from Trubetzkoy (Cairns 1972:922):

```
                  v   z
              x   f   s   š
      p   t   k   p̌   c
      b   d   g
      m   n   ŋ
```

                (Trubetzkoy 1939:64)

This diagram permutes both columns (the usual
order of which follows the oral cavity) and rows.
It is thereby a better fit for the data, the
system of correlations:

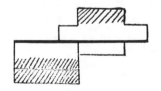

(Sounds above the heavy line are fricatives;
sounds in shaded areas are voiced.)

None of these differences, however, alters the meaning of matrix diagrams. The juxtaposition of the two dimensions, the cell as a locus at the intersection of the two dimensions, carry the same meaning. But the second type of matrix diagram, which we have called the grid, *is* different; though it, like the matrix diagrams we have looked at, expresses componential analysis, it construes the graphic elements of the matrix in a different way.

Componential analysis in a grid

An example of a grid is Halle's representation for the sounds of Russian--a translation, in fact, of the key reproduced in the last chapter:

```
              j t d t, d, n n, c s z s, z, p b p, b, m m, f v f, v,
vocalic       - - - -  - -  - - - - -  -  - - -  -  - -  - - -  -
consonantal   - + + +  + +  + + + + +  +  + + +  +  + +  + + +  +
diffuse       o o o o  o o  o o o o o  o  o o o  o  o o  o o o  o
compact       o - - -  - -  - - - - -  -  - - -  -  - -  - - -  -
low tonality  o - - -  - -  - - - - -  +  + + +  +  + +  + + +  +
strident      o - - -  - -  - + + + +  +  - - -  -  - -  + + +  +
nasal         o - - -  - +  + o o o o  o  - - -  -  + +  o o o  o
continuant    o o o o  o o  o - + + +  +  o o o  o  o o  o o o  o
voiced        o - + -  + o  o o - + -  +  - + -  +  o o  - + -  +
sharped       o - - +  + -  + o - - +  +  - - +  +  - +  - - +  +
accented      o o o o  o o  o o o o o  o  o o o  o  o o  o o o  o


              č š ž k k, g x e 'e o 'o a 'a i 'i u 'u r r, l l,
vocalic       - - - - -  - -  + + +  + +  + +  + +  + +  + +
consonantal   + + + + +  + +  - - -  - -  - -  - -  + +  + +
diffuse       o o o o o  o o  - - -  - -  - +  + +  + o o  o o
compact       + + + + +  + +  - - -  - +  + o  o o  o o  o o
low tonality  - - - + +  + +  - - +  + o  o -  - +  + o o  o o
strident      o o o o o  o o  o o o  o o  o o  o o  o o  o o
nasal         o o o o o  o o  o o o  o o  o o  o o  o o  o o
continuant    - + + - -  - +  o o o  o o  o o  o o  o -  - + +
voiced        o - + - -  + o  o o o  o o  o o  o o  o o  o o
sharped       o o o - +  o o  o o o  o o  o o  o o  o -  + - +
accented      o o o o o  o o  - + -  + -  + -  + -  + o o  o o
```

(Halle 1959:45)

A grid has the graphic elements of a matrix but construes them differently. Rows, in the grid as

in the matrix, represent features; columns, however, represent not features but sets of feature
specifications, and a cell contains not a unit of
the sound system, but a partial specification of
a unit. The intersection of the two dimensions
no longer defines a whole entity, but simply characterizes one entity, a sound, with respect to
another, a feature:

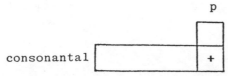

The stuff of the matrix--the units of the sound
system--has been moved out to the periphery.
     Why this rearrangement? It allows represen-
tation of combinations of more than two features
at a time. If the units of a sound system fill
the cells, a unit is the product of two and only
two features, one on each dimension. (Often, it is
true, manner of articulation combines more than
one feature--say, [±Voice] and [±Continuant]: these
we shall consider portmanteau features and treat
as single features.) If, on the other hand, the
units of a sound system are deployed along the
periphery, there is theoretically no limit to the
number of features specifying a unit. This gain
is offset by a greater loss. In a grid, an empty
cell signifies no more than the fact that part of
the specification of a sound is dispensable; and
the boundary of a grid cannot be invested with
meaning. Because nothing can be placed outside
the figure, because the figure has no end, the dichotomy between inside and outside vanishes. The
contrasts on which the matrix is founded--the
juxtaposing of rows and columns, of full and empty
cells, of inside and outside--are not exploited in
the grid. And at the same time that it fails
to exploit these graphic elements, the grid requires additional graphic devices. Labelling is
essential: one cannot take soundings by the
values filling the cells to find out the meaning
of the dimensions.

The net effect of these changes in the meaning
of the graphic elements is that the figure no
longer says the same thing. Shifting the units of
the sound system from center to periphery means
the figure no longer makes its statement about
them. What fills the cells is the topic of the
figure: in the grid it is not the sounds, not the
features, but the values of the features.

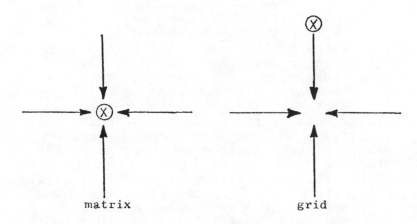

matrix   grid

Both the inventory and the pattern of sounds are
thus relegated to a lesser place. The grid in
fact gains the capacity to specify a theoretically
infinite number of features and to define a theoretically infinite number of sounds, at the
expense of its capacity to represent pattern.
A grid is less a graphic representation than a
list. It is simply a list that happens to be
in two dimensions, stretching across the page as
well as down.
      Expanding the chart of figures and meanings
to accommodate matrix diagrams (recalling that
matrix and grid are simply different expressions
of the same meaning) gives us

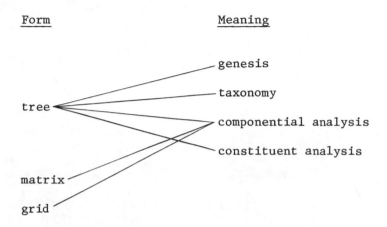

Form   Meaning

tree

matrix

grid

genesis

taxonomy

componential analysis

constituent analysis

Now besides the homonymy exhibited by tree dia-
grams--one figure expressing four meanings--we
have synonymy as well; for matrix diagrams and
tree diagrams both express componential analysis.
The correspondence between form and meaning for
graphic representation in linguistics become even
more tangled when we consider still another kind
of diagram.

Box diagrams

Besides tree diagrams and matrix diagrams, there is another sort of diagram in linguistics that is not so easily catalogued. Box diagrams are a more elusive quarry, for what we shall group under the heading of box diagrams are really three different figures. They are usually called cubes, Chinese box diagrams, and block diagrams; they are constructions making use of shape or area rather than (like tree and matrix diagrams) of line. Their provenience is less interesting than the provenience of tree and matrix diagrams; and it is various. We shall therefore leave it to be touched on in connection with each of the three figures.

Meaning

The meaning of box diagrams is the relation of parts of a system to each other and to the whole. They are structures built of rectangles (see following page). Each kind of box diagram assembles the parts--rectangles--into a whole in its own way. The relation of areas to each other in space expresses the relation of parts in a system. This most abstract meaning, the meaning of box diagrams as a graphic design, is converted in any given instance into one of three more specific meanings, depending on how the graphic elements of the design are construed.

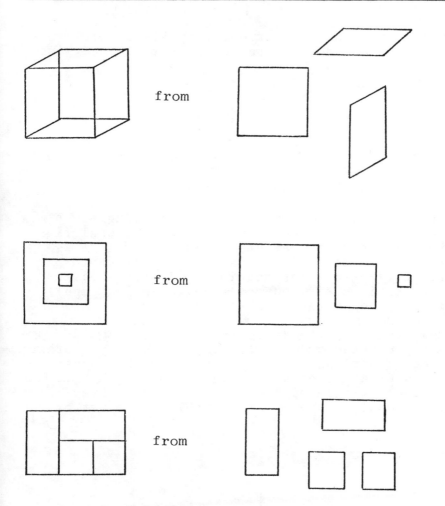

Two of them we have met before: componential analysis and constituent analysis; the third meaning we shall call conflation.

Componential analysis in a cube

As for its provenience, Forchhammer employed the cube, in what was probably its first appearance in linguistics, as early as 1924 (Forchhammer 1924:42). Gleason's cube for the Turkish vowel

system, however, is for our purposes a more repre-
sentative box diagram for componential analysis:

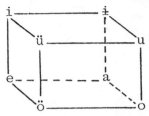

(Gleason 1961:267)

Cube diagrams are constructed of rectangles in
such a way as to convey a three-dimensional figure, and in this they are unlike any figure we
have looked at so far. Their illusory depth--
perspective--carries meaning. Gleason's diagram
resolves into six squares (see following page).
Illusory depth reassembles the six areas into a
whole. We view the figure as six congruent shapes
projected to three different planes. Vowel height
is represented by one plane; rounding, by another;
place of articulation, by a third. The opposite
values of a component--[+High] *versus* [-High], for
instance--are on opposite sides of the three-
dimensional figure. This establishes a set of
axes:

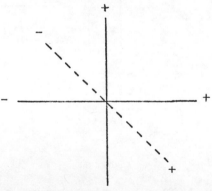

The similarity of the six sides now reflects the
uniformity of the stuff of the figure, phonetic

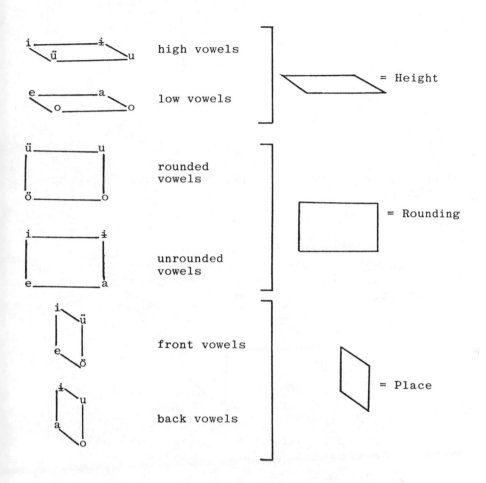

components; the difference in plane reflects the
distinctness of phonetic components one from
another. The opposition of two sides in a plane
reflects the polarity of the two values of a
component, plus and minus.

Plane opposes plane to express components:
pole opposes pole to express values of components.
This is perhaps more evident in Hockett's version
of the diagram for Turkish vowels:

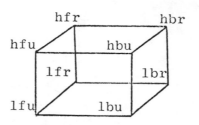

(Hockett 1958:96)

Here the set of points sharing one and only one component,

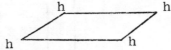

can be spanned, without travelling along the axes, by a single square. The set of points sharing no component,

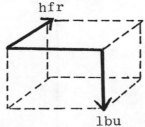

can be spanned only by travelling along all three axes. The greatest distance between two points corresponds to the greatest difference between two units in the system.

Like the matrix, then, the cube expresses the pattern as well as the inventory of a sound system. The two figures are partly isomorphic. The cells of the matrix are the corners of the cube. The rows and columns of the matrix are the sides of the cube. The dimensions of the matrix are the dimensions of the cube--and therein lies the difference between the two figures. While the matrix represents a unit as the intersection

of two dimensions, the cube represents it as the
intersection of three: the matrix analyzes a unit
as the product of two features; the cube, as the
product of three. We may therefore expect the
cube to replace the matrix when the componential
analysis of a system requires three features
rather than two.

This is not quite what happens in Jakobson's
(1958) componential analysis of the Russian case
system. The three features are: [±Directional]
(*napravlennost'*); [±Quantitative] (*objemnost'*);
[±Peripheral] (*periferijnost'*). A grid for
Jakobson's first version of a distinctive-feature
analysis of the Russian case system, in which the
number of cases is six, would look like this:

	Nom	Acc	Dat	Gen	Prep	Inst
Directional	−	+	+	0	0	−
Quantitative	−	−	−	+	+	−
Peripheral	−	−	+	−	+	+

Two more cases--the "second genitive" (Gen$_2$) and
the "second accusative" (Prep$_2$)--are then added.
A grid for this second version, in which the number of cases has grown from six to eight, would
look like this:

	Nom	Acc	Dat	Gen$_1$	Gen$_2$	Prep$_1$	Prep$_2$	Inst
Directional	−	+	+	+	−	+	−	−
Quantitative	−	−	−	+	+	+	+	−
Peripheral	−	−	+	−	−	+	+	+

For eight cases, the two "holes" in the grid are
filled in, so that all features are specified
for all cases. With this change in inventory
comes a change in pattern. For a six-case analysis, the pattern in which the cases stand can
be represented by a matrix. The matrix underlying Jakobson's analysis is:

Nominative	Accusative	Genitive
Instrumental	Dative	Prepositional- Locative

But when the number of cases grows from six to
eight, so that all three features are distinctive
for every case, the matrix is stretched and pulled
into a cube:

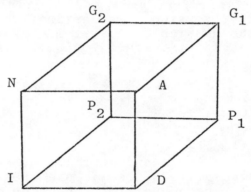

(Jakobson: 1963:149
[Roman letters replace Cyrillic])

There is no change in the number of features,
only in the number of features that are distinctive in every case.
      A three-feature analysis, then, is necessary
but not sufficient for the matrix to give way to
the cube. Is it that the three features must be
distinctive for every unit in the system? Must
there be no unused feature combinations (properly
speaking, permutations)--no empty cells in either
a matrix or a grid for the system? But this is
not a sufficient condition either; for in cubes
like this one,

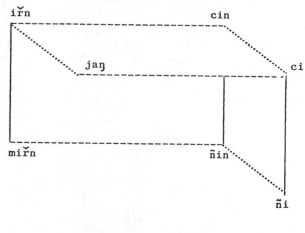

(Austerlitz 1959:105)

there is clearly one combination of features, at
any rate, that goes unused, and that is the one
that would occupy the missing corner. In the
cube, as in the matrix, empty corners are as
meaningful as full ones, though there are limits
to this. Jakobson's first version of the Russian
case system might, it is true, have been shown in
the fashion of Austerlitz's diagram:

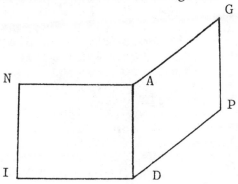

But this looks odd: it has an uneasy disproportion.
     Again like the matrix, the cube can be made
to accommodate, within the limits set by the componential analysis it represents, more sounds than
it necessarily shows. Unlike the matrix, however,
the cube at first sight looks like a different figure when it is so expanded. Jespersen's representation of the Danish vowel system, for example,

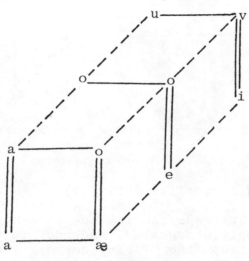

(Jespersen 1934:104)

appears to be a double cube. It is actually the
expansion of a binary analysis to *n*-ary. "Stretching" the cube accommodates three degrees of vowel
height instead of two. The cube is, in fact,
infinitely elastic. Its expansion, mathematically
formalizable, can accommodate a theoretically
infinite number of feature values, and therefore
of sounds (see figure from Kay and Romney, following page). But it cannot increase the number
of features by a single one.
     The limit is set by the design. Because it
is a three-dimensional configuration, the figure
itself sets the number of features at three and
only three. Its expansion in no way changes the
cube into another figure; the expansion of the

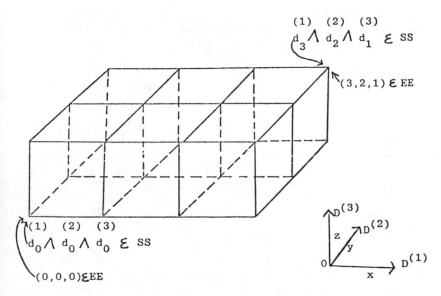

(Kay and Romney 1967:8)

number of possible feature-values in no way
changes the three-feature analysis.

Constituent analysis in box diagrams

The meaning of constituent analysis is
expressed by two different box diagrams: Chinese
box diagrams and block diagrams. The Chinese box,
named by Francis (1958:293), looks like this:

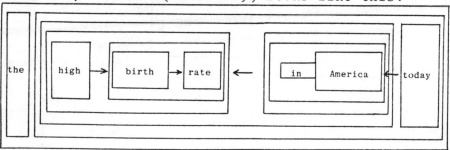

(Francis 1958:312)

Of its provenience, Francis says (personal communication) that it derives from the representation for
immediate constituent analysis used by Fries (1952),

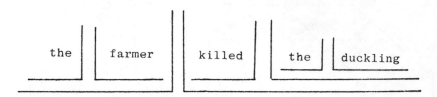

by "filling in the tops":

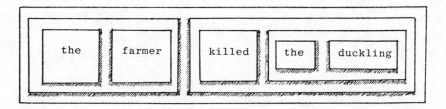

　　Chinese boxes are constructed of rectangles
in such a way as to show the relationship of
inclusion by graphic inclusion. The inclusion of
one element in another--a constituent--and the
inclusion by one element of another--a construc-
tion--are shown as the inclusion of areas in
space. One rectangle is seen as containing or
contained by another, allowing

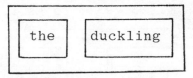

to be read as at once

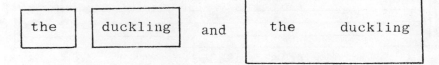

The second sort of box diagram for constituent
analysis is almost, but not quite, a Chinese box.

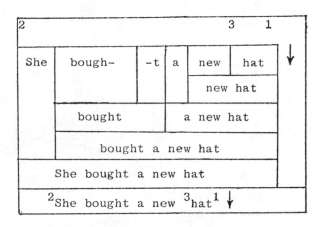

(Hockett 1958:158)

This is what we have called, following Nida (1964),
a block diagram. That it, too, is constructed of
rectangles is more easily seen from Hockett's
"empty box" for the same sentence:

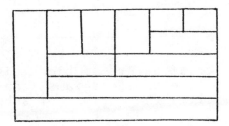

(Hockett 1958:159 [suprasegmentals omitted])

A construction--*new hat*, for instance--is represented by means of areas related in space. This
relatedness of areas in space is accomplished,
not by the illusion of depth, as in the cube, but
by exploiting the linearity of the two-dimensional
page. We begin with six elements, *she*, *bough-*,
-t, *a*, *new*, and *hat*. These are then progressively

amalgamated by welding two areas into a single
area. So *new* and *hat* become *new hat*, which is
thereupon joined by *a*; and these two are amalgamated into *a new hat*; and so on.

The serial nature of the block diagram
recalls the tree.

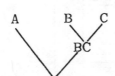
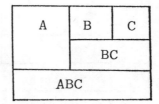

And it is true that the two are isomorphic. Nodes
correspond to rectangles; branches, to the size
and position of rectangles:

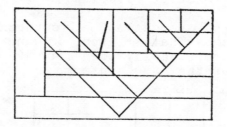

Moreover, the serial nature of block diagrams is
such that they, like tree diagrams, can be made
to convey explicitly the notions of substituta-
bility:

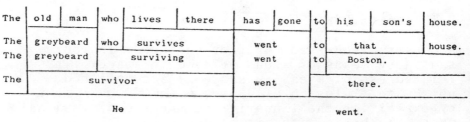

(Gleason 1961:130)

and constituent function:

Subject-Predicate Sentence					
Noun Phrase			Verb phrase		
Article	Noun Phrase		Verb	Prepositional phrase	
	Adj.	Noun		Prep.	Pronoun
The	old	men	stared	at	us.

(Nida 1964:38)

None of this, however, alters the fact that block diagrams are graphically box diagrams, and not trees at all. They are close kin to Chinese boxes. The representation from which the Chinese box derives,

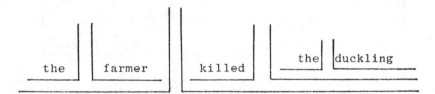

can with just as little tinkering serve to derive the block diagram:

the	farmer	killed	the	duckling

This time it is not a matter of filling in the tops but rather of making boundaries common boundaries, so that abutting rectangles share a boundary. The two sorts of box diagram used for

constituent analysis, then, are similar figures
with the same origin. Block diagrams for the
meaning of conflation have a different origin.

Conflation

The block diagram for the meaning of constituent analysis, as we have seen, can be matched
with a tree. There is, as well, a block diagram
for the meaning of conflation, which can be
matched with a matrix.

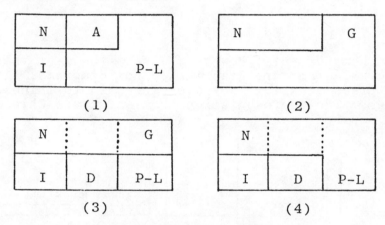

(Jakobson 1958:136-140
[Roman letters replace Cyrillic])

These figures display patterns of case conflation
against an "understood" matrix.[7] This is the
matrix proposed earlier,

Nominative	Accusative	Genitive
Instrumental	Dative	Prepositional-Locative

This matrix, as we have said, expresses a componential analysis of the case system of Russian,

with three distinctive features, [±Directional],
[±Quantitative], [±Peripheral]. Comparison with
an understood matrix is what gives conflation diagrams their meaning. The position and shape of
the rectangles (of course, not all the blocks in
such diagrams are, properly speaking, rectangles)
signals the flowing together of certain formerly
distinct entities. To show conflation requires
the graphic elements not only of the block diagram, but also of the matrix. Rectangles are
plotted on the matrix as the aggregate of certain
cells (the area encompassing the Prepositional-
Locative ending is not the same for Jakobson's
Figure 1 as for Figure 2, showing that it is conflated with different case endings in the two
systems). Empty space signifies absence just as
in the matrix (the Accusative ending does not
occur for the paradigm represented by Figure 3).
The boundary of the conflation diagram is not
significant, but boundaries between cells are:
removal of the boundary between abutting cells
indicates irreversible conflation (of Accusative
with Nominative, in Figure 2); a permeable bound-
ary--shown by dotted lines--indicates a case sub-
sumed now under one, now under another ending
(the Accusative in Figures 3 and 4).
     The block diagram for conflation, then, is
composed of figure (the conflated system) and
ground (the implied matrix for a full system).
Unlike the block diagram for immediate constituent
analysis--or the matrix itself, for that matter--
the block diagram for conflation is not static.
The contrast between the conflated system and the
full system gives conflation diagrams an ineluc-
table element of process, of change. Pike's diagram for suspicious pairs in phonological analysis
perhaps shows this more clearly (see following
page). Sounds enclosed in a ring are suspicious--
that is, they are likely to be allophones of a
single phoneme; if they are, they are conflated.
Pike's diagram is a sort of blueprint of all
possible conflated systems that might occur,
given this particular full underlying matrix.

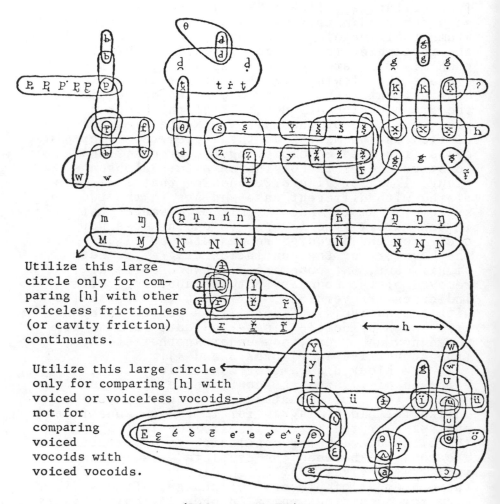

Utilize this large
circle only for com-
paring [h] with other
voiceless frictionless
(or cavity friction)
continuants.

Utilize this large circle
only for comparing [h] with
voiced or voiceless vocoids—
not for
comparing
voiced
vocoids with
voiced vocoids.

(Pike 1947:70)

The full system expressed by the implicit
matrix that underlies a conflation diagram need
not, strictly speaking, be an earlier stage of
the conflated system. It can be simply the
fully-specified system of contrasts implicit
in the feature analysis itself:

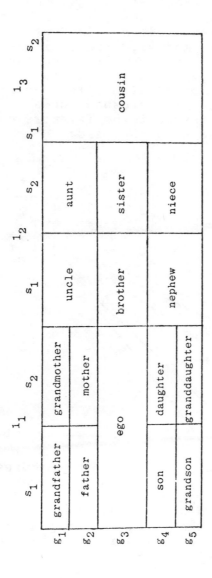

(Nida 1964:85)

Here *ego* conflates the two theoretically possible
feature combinations $[l_1\ s_1\ g_3]$ and $[l_1\ s_2\ g_3]$;
uncle, aunt, nephew, and *niece* each conflate two
possible combinations; *cousin* conflates ten. The
underlying full matrix, here as in Jakobson's diagrams, is easily inferred from the conflated matrix
because it is implicit in the feature analysis.
    In the taxonomy of diagrams in linguistics
proposed here, the correspondences between form
and meaning are seen to be far more complicated
than might have been supposed:

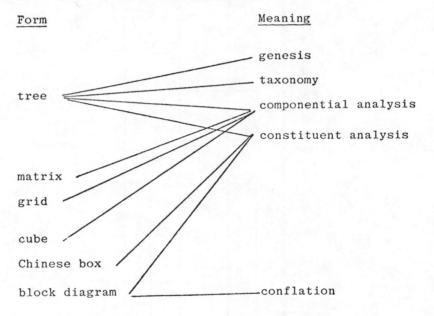

The relationship between form--figures--and
meaning--analytic techniques--is, as we have said,
far from isomorphic. All of the figures are
synonyms for some meaning: the tree, the matrix,
the grid, and the cube, for componential analysis;
the tree, the Chinese box, and the block diagram,
for constituent analysis. Conversely, two of the
figures are homonyms: the tree, for genesis,
taxonomy, componential analysis, and constituent
analysis; the block diagram, for constituent

analysis and conflation. Synonymy and homonymy
tangle the correspondences between form and
meaning. This, then, is the situation in linguistics at present. What is its significance
for linguistic science?

Graphic representation and linguistic science

We have seen that it is entirely possible to speak of graphic representation as a distinct element in linguistic science; but what is important about the existence of three basic figures? What is their role in the development of linguistic science? To see where graphic representation fits into the structure of linguistic science, we must have recourse to the philosophy of science, the first of our two perspectives on graphic representation in linguistics.

Graphic representation and the philosophy of science

Any discussion of graphic representation in linguistic science has for its context the philosophy of science; for the nature, place, and function of graphic representation are determined by, and in turn determine, other components of linguistic science. Some sort of working definition, then, of such notions as "theory," "law," and "model" is indispensable. Indeed, a working definition is the most that can be aspired to: the philosophy of science is a field (as Tennyson put it) whose margin fades forever and forever when we move. The definitions arrived at here, based on an eclectic, often expedient survey of the philosophy of science, are shaped to the discussion of graphic representation that follows.

There is controversy among philosophers of
science even over what constitutes a scientific
theory. Nagel (1961:117-152) discusses three different conceptions of scientific theory: "descriptive," "instrumentalist," and "realist." These
are differences in orientation toward science itself. The instrumentalist view is particularly
useful for graphic representation and for linguistic science in general. Toulmin (1953:108),
for instance, sees scientific theory as a map in
which

> the diagrams present all that is contained in
> the set of observational statements, but do so
> in a logically novel manner: the aggregate of
> discrete observations is transformed into a
> simple and connected picture.

Such a view is an eminently sensible conception of
the relationship between theory and reality. Although map-making demands *a priori* choices--the
cartographer's choice of method of projection,
scale, and so forth--which render subjective a
scientist's-eye view of reality, "the alternative
. . . is not a truer map [but] no map at all"
(Toulmin, 127). The instrumentalist position is
captured in Hadamard's (1945:xi-xii) characterization of scientific theory as invention rather
than discovery.
    We shall assume here, then, that a scientific
theory is an artifice. Some further distinctions,
largely irrelevant to a consideration of graphic
representation, will not be taken up here. These
are such questions as whether a theory constitutes
description or explanation (Toulmin 1953:53);
which of the various types of explanation--deduc-
tive, probabilistic, functional or teleological,
genetic--a theory exhibits (Nagel, 20-26); whether
explanation follows the "pattern model" or the
"deductive model" (Kaplan 1964:332-338).
    The distinction between theory and law (Nagel,
64-67) is, in linguistics, hard to discern. Does
Grimm's Law, for instance, constitute a theory of

sound change, as would seem to be the case when it
is set beside the theory of Martinet (1955)? Or
is it a law? If it is a law, what is its scope?
If its scope is not restricted to the past, it is
a poor law, for the phenomenon by no means invari-
ably occurs (Nagel, 63; but cf. Campbell 1921:69).
Moreover, linguistic science has not yet reached
the point where "universals" are verifiable, if
indeed they are useful at all. If, on the other
hand, the scope of Grimm's Law is restricted to
the past--a reconstructed past, at that--it is
not a law at all (Nagel, 63, but cf. Campbell,69).
Yet it surely goes beyond description, though it
falls short of explanation.

        Less dispensable than a definition of theory
or law is a definition of model. For one thing,
as Chao (1962) has demonstrated, the term "model"
covers a whole flock of senses, which fly off in
different directions when approached too closely;
for another, graphic representation and models
are (as we shall see) closely connected. The
place of the model within scientific theory must
be established first of all. Not unexpectedly,
philosophers of science disagree: their conceptions range from an indispensable and even pre-
theoretic model to a peripheral, purely decorative
one.[8] Again the middle ground will serve us best;
and again Toulmin's conception is useful. Beside
his notion of the theory as a map we may set
Toulmin's assertion (1953:35) that models supple-
ment theory by providing a "clearly intelligible
way of conceiving the physical systems we study."
A model, then, is the bridge between "discrete
observations" about the data and the "simple and
connected picture" furnished by a theory.

        The function of the model standing midway
between data and theory is to mediate between the
very concrete and the very abstract. An example
is the wave theory of light. This theory provides a concrete, visualizable model--water waves--
for an abstract mathematical formulation of the
properties of light. It does so by means of the
similarities between water and light; by means of

the correspondences between a known thing and the
unknown datum, the *explicandum*; by means, in short,
of analogy. This notion of the relationship between model and data is formulated by Hesse (1966:
68-69) as "material analogy," a relationship in
which the similarity between terms of the analogue
and corresponding terms of the *explicandum* is independent of causal relations within each.[9] For the
wave theory of light, the likeness of the model to
the *explicandum* can be elaborated in the following
way (Hesse, 11):

WATER WAVES	LIGHT
Produced by motion of water particles	Produced by moving flame, etc.
Properties of reflection	Reflection in mirrors, etc.
Properties of diffraction	Diffraction through small slits, etc.
Amplitude	Brightness
Frequency	Color
Medium: Water	Medium: "Ether"

Each term of the analogue, water waves, serves to
explain, translate, render visualizable, some
aspect of the *explicandum*, light.
     Models, however, not only serve but also
influence theory. These two functions--the interpretive and the heuristic--are in some measure
attributed to models by nearly all philosophers
of science.[10] Like the interpretive function,
which we have been discussing, the heuristic function of models is rooted in material analogy The
heuristic usefulness of the model, its usefulness
in extending and developing a scientific theory,
depends upon the incompleteness of the analogy;
that is, the likeness of model to *explicandum*
must constitute a material analogy only for some
terms, leaving others still to be explored. Thus
if we go on spinning out the correspondences between water waves and light, we eventually arrive
at such likenesses as

WATER WAVES	LIGHT
Density of medium	Ether density
Elasticity of medium	Ether elasticity

These two correspondences are at the outset part of what Hesse calls the "neutral analogy"--elements of the model whose relevance for the *explicandum* is unknown. It is by virtue of the neutral analogy that a model furnishes suggestions for the development of a scientific theory. As it happens, neither ether density nor ether elasticity is a significant property of the medium in which light is propagated; these terms are accordingly relegated to the "negative analogy"--elements of the model irrelevant for the *explicandum*. Had they turned out to be significant, they would have been incorporated into the "positive analogy"--elements of the model relevant for the *explicandum*--along with frequency, amplitude, and so on. The heuristic function of models consists in the exploration of the neutral analogy, which develops and extends the scientific theory: it adds to or elaborates the positive analogy and at the same time circumscribes it, sets its boundaries, by establishing the negative analogy.

Form follows function. If the model is to perform an interpretive function with respect to the abstract formal theory--to constitute, in effect, a translation of the theory--model and theory must be isomorphic. Explicitly suggested by such theorists as Black (1962:238) and Kaplan (1964:263), this is implicit in any notion of model. If the model is to perform a heuristic function, it must be a partial isomorph for the *explicandum*, as well.

The model, then, is a Janus-like thing, whose place is midway between theory and *explicandum*; whose function is at once interpretive and heuristic; whose form is an isomorph in two directions. In a chronology of theory formation, the model may make its appearance before the formal theory has assumed its final shape--

perhaps even prior to any formal theory. What
then is the place of graphic representation in
scientific theory? We have said that it is hard
to apply the concept of scientific law to linguistic science. Most linguistic statements that
are called laws (Grimm's Law, Grassmann's Law,
Verner's Law) will not, because they characterize
events past or unique, meet the standards for
scientific laws. Yet they are not simple description: they structure the data. Often this structure is expressed in a graphic configuration, like
the figure for Grimm's Law, the *Kreislauf* (not,
in fact, Grimm's design but Schleicher's [1888:
97]). For linguistics, the closest thing to a
scientific law is the statement of a discovered
(better, an invented) regularity, often graphically
expressed.
      Similarly, the concept of model, even the
relatively capacious one of the model as analogue,
will not fit linguistic science without alteration.
Models presented as such are rare in linguistics--
perhaps because it has had relatively little use,
compared with physics or biology, for physical
scale models, and less awareness therefore of the
model as an element in scientific theory. Moreover, explicit models--the computer in descriptive linguistics (Yngve 1966), human genealogy in
historical linguistics--cannot be expected to
serve as what Harré (1960:105) calls "candidates-
for-reality." There is no hope of someday vali-
dating the model by discovering it to be an actual
physical structure, like the double helix in biology. Implicit models, however, abound: when
graphic representation accompanies a linguistic
statement, an unexpressed "is like" couples picture and prose. For linguistics, the notion of
model, like the notion of scientific law, is
accessible by way of graphic representation. It
is as a model that a figure can come to have a
life of its own--can, in fact, like models in
science generally, influence the theory out of
which it grew. This is sometimes obscured by the

prominence of a detailed, highly structured theory
that is assumed to govern the model; but, as we
shall see, linguistic theory is often demonstrably
the product of its representation.

The influence of graphic representation
on linguistic theory

        A notion may be fleeting, doubtful, vague;
once it is codified as a method of representation,
a figure, it must be reckoned with in all its
implacable detail. Graphic representation influences scientific theory in two ways: in its
extension, and in its development.[11] The extension
of a theory is its application to more kinds of
data than that for which it originated; the development of a theory is its articulation in progressively greater detail, and its modification. The
more negotiable a figure--the more readily the
design applies to various kinds of data--the more
it facilitates the extension of linguistic theory.
The more suggestive a figure--the more avenues
for further exploration the design unfolds--the
more it contributes to the development of
linguistic theory.

The extension of linguistic theory

        The matrix illustrates extension. That the
matrix is a negotiable figure is demonstrated by
its transfer from traditional articulatory phonetics to distinctive feature analysis; from
phonology to morphology to semantics. The theory
of componential analysis is thereby extended to
practically every aspect of language. For phonology, as we have seen, matrix arrangement and
componential analysis are indispensable. For
morphology, besides Jakobson's matrix arrangement
and distinctive feature analysis for case (Jakobson 1958, a much earlier version of which is
Jakobson 1936), there are Sebeok's (1946) for case

and Jakobson's (1957) and Joos's (1964) for con-
jugation. For semantics, besides the semantic
theory of Katz and Fodor incorporated by transformational-generative grammar (Katz and Postal 1964),
there are componential analyses in linguistics
(Austerlitz 1959, Nida 1964) and in anthropology
(Colby 1966, Kay 1969).
     Pike (1962) attests the transfer of graphic
representation *per se* and its effect on the
extension of theory. He asks (221),

> Can grammatical dimensions be charted like
> phonetic ones? . . . for grammar, what would
> be the analogy of

$$p \quad t \quad k$$
$$b \quad d \quad g$$
$$m \quad n \quad \eta$$

The matrix, then, is a negotiable figure indeed.
The effect of its negotiability on the extension
of the theory of componential analysis is plain.
     The tree is also a negotiable figure; but
its effect on the extension of linguistic theory
is less happy. On the transfer of the figure itself, little need be said. We have already seen
the negotiability of the tree in its migration
from diachronic to synchronic linguistics; from
structural linguistics to transformational-generative grammar; from syntax to phonology to semantics. Its itinerary is of interest for the
extension of linguistic theory, and it is for
this reason that we considered at length the
provenience of tree diagrams. The negotiability
of the tree is such, indeed, that the notion that
"Chomsky got his tree from Schleicher" is not so
absurd as Maher (1966:9) makes it sound.
     How does the transfer of the figure effect
the extension of linguistic theory? Not of a
single theory; for the tree cannot--any more than
the matrix, which comprises such diverse analytic
techniques as taxonomic (articulatory) phonemics
and generative phonology--be said to correspond
to a single theory. With the spread of the tree

there has, however, been the spread of a theoretical bias--what Holton (1964) calls a thema. The
thema for the tree is its most general meaning:
subordination, expressed, quite literally, by "placing under." Whatever its modification, the figure
carries this theme, as the matrix carries the theme
of componential analysis. (They are the two great
themes of linguistic science, deriving ultimately
from the same principle: divide and conquer.)
But we have said that extension of theory--exten-
sion, that is, of the theme of subordination--is,
in the case of the tree, unwarranted. If the
measure of extension is the number of meanings
conveyed by a figure, the measure of unwarranted-
ness is the confusion that results. The chart at
the end of the last chapter shows the extent of
the synonymy and homonymy in which the meanings
of the tree take part. Several diverse techniques
of linguistic analysis employ the tree, often in
more than one of its meanings. So wide an application of the figure has resulted in the accretion
of conflicting meanings; they become impossible to
dislodge, creating confusion, contradiction, ambiguity. To the extent that any given tree diagram
provokes this confusion, the transfer of the
figure has ended in unwarranted extension.

The development of linguistic theory

The negotiability of a method of representation influences the extension of a theory, widens
it, as it were; the suggestiveness of a method of
representation influences its development, deepens
it. A heuristic value for the development of
theory is taken for granted in discussions like
that of Pike (1962:240) concerning the applica-
bility of the matrix arrangement to grammar. It
sounds as if the subject were some new piece of
laboratory equipment:

> a set of preliminary dimension charts for
> grammatical constructions helps the consultant

> to alert the beginner to gaps in his data by
> allowing him to see more clearly the over-all
> grammatical structural system.

Sebeok (1946:18) makes a similar claim for its
application to case. The matrix arrangement, he
says, "will make comparison of the Finnish with
other systems visually feasible and will also
reveal certain structural characteristics of Finnish itself." Hockett's apologia (1958:109) gives
this use of graphic representation a name, the
"principle of neatness of pattern." "If we are
confronted with two or more ways of identifying
allophones as phonemes, both or all of which
equally well meet all other criteria," he says,
"we should choose that alternative which yields
the most symmetrical portrayal of the system."
And Trubetzkoy himself claimed for the matrix a
more than decorative import (1939:65; quoted in
Cairns 1972:123):

> die Ordnung, die durch Aufteilung der Phoneme
> in parallele Reihen erreicht wird, existiert
> nicht nur auf dem Papier und is nicht bloss
> eine graphische Angelegenheit. Sie entspricht
> vielmehr einer phonologischen Realität.

Graphic representation--at least, the matrix dia-
gram--is seen not as a mere embellishment but as
a tool.
     There are many more instances in which such
a view is implicit. Jakobson's diagrams for case
conflation, which we looked at earlier, in fact
parlay the matrix into a theory of case conflation. The "conflated field structures" of Pike
and Erickson (1964) are the mirror image of
Jakobson's procedure: the whole search for pattern in the data consists simply in inspection
and rearrangement. The use of such structures
asserts that sheer scrutiny of the data can
render it intelligible, if matrix arrangement is
the lens through which it is viewed.
     The suggestiveness of graphic representation
has played a role in historical linguistics from

its beginnings. Considerations of pattern and
symmetry are more pressing when it is a matter of
reconstruction, because there is not the counter-
balance of an actually existing system in all its
unruliness. Saussure's famous monograph of 1879
apparently rests upon such a use of matrix
arrangement.
        Graphic representation can also work the di-
rect development of linguistic theory, without
going by way of the data. We have mentioned the
transfer of the matrix from traditional articulatory phonetics to distinctive feature theory.
In both, it has proved to be productive for the
development of theory. In both, the development
is from a synchronic theory into a diachronic
theory. The traditional articulatory matrix
grounds Austin's (1957) theory of sound change,
which says that sounds shift by travelling along
the horizontal or vertical, never the diagonal.
Thus a sound x cannot become y in fewer than two
moves. We can express this as

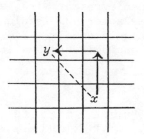

The matrix arrangement underlying Martinet's (1955)
theory of sound change is that of distinctive
feature analysis. But the theory has the same
components as Austin's: movement and direction;
and phonological space is the backdrop against
which the diachronic drama is played out. Martinet gives no figure, but one from King (1967:3)
can serve:

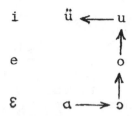

Both Austin's and Martinet's conceptions of sound
change grow out of the matrix figure. The components of the diachronic theory, movement and direction, can be traced to the figure as convincingly
as to the synchronic theory.

It is illuminating to set beside the theories
of Austin and Martinet a third, much earlier conception of sound change as movement against a
matrix. This is Anton Pfalz's (1918) notion of
Reihenschritte. Vowels that are the same in vowel
height undergo the same change: if [i] becomes
[ei], [u] becomes [ou]. In other words, sounds in
the same row in a matrix arrangement behave in the
same way. Pfalz lists the sound changes governed
by this principle in what is itself a matrix
arrangement:

Wo der	*i*-Laut	>	*è*	wird,	wird der	*u*-Laut	>	*ȯ*	
"	"	*i*-Laut	>	*ę*	"	"	"	*u*-Laut	>	*ǫ*
"	"	*i*-Laut	>	*i̦i*	"	"	"	*u*-Laut	>	*u̦u*
"	"	*i*-Laut	>	*ei*	"	"	"	*u*-Laut	>	*ou*
"	"	*i*-Laut	>	*äi̦*	"	"	"	*u*-Laut	>	*åu̦.*
Wo der	*e*-Laut	>	*ę*	wird,	wird der	*o*-Laut	>	*ǫ*	
"	"	*e*-Laut	>	*i*	"	"	"	*o*-Laut	>	*u*
"	"	*e*-Laut	>	*ęv*	"	"	"	*o*-Laut	>	*ǫv*
"	"	*e*-Laut	>	*ęə*	"	"	"	*o*-Laut	>	*ǫə*
"	"	*e*-Laut	>	*ęi̦*	"	"	"	*o*-Laut	>	*ǫu̦*
"	"	*e*-Laut	>	*èi*	"	"	"	*o*-Laut	>	*ȯu*
"	"	*e*-Laut	>	*ię́*	"	"	"	*o*-Laut	>	*uǫ́.*

(Pfalz 1918:28)

Here the matrix figure clearly directs the choreo-
graphy of vowel change.
    The process by which a figure effects the
development of linguistic theory is the process
by which a model effects the development of any
scientific theory. It is the exploration of the
neutral analogy. In all three theories of sound
change, the matrix figure has furnished the neutral analogy for the development of a diachronic
theory out of a synchronic one; the route from one
to the other is by way of the neutral analogy--by
investigating aspects of the model, the matrix
figure, whose relevance for the explicandum, sound
change, is not known. Out of them, the two dimensions, horizontal and vertical, have been assigned
to the positive analogy; while the figure's static
quality has been assigned to the negative analogy,
to be replaced by the notion of sound change as
sound movement. For Martinet's theory, exploration of the neutral analogy yields in addition the
notions case vide, marge de sécurité, champ de
dispersion, chaîne de propulsion, chaîne de trac-
tion. A case vide is of course an empty cell;
marge de sécurité is suggested by the boundaries
between cells; champ de dispersion is the flat
ground or "field" furnished by the matrix; and a
chain-like progress of sounds across the matrix
is the only conceivable sort. The notion of
chaîne includes only the columns of the matrix
figure, however; rows are relegated to the negative analogy, inasmuch as position on the horizontal dimension has little significance for sound
change (Martinet, personal communication).
    The theories of Austin, Martinet, and Pfalz
all illustrate the development of a synchronic
theory into a diachronic one. Another direction
suggested by the matrix analogue for the development of linguistic theory is illustrated by the
work of Pike. Here the matrix suggests a finished
theory that outgrows the matrix figure. Thus the
following figure,

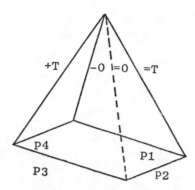

(Pike 1962:235)

translates the outgrown matrix:

	P_1	P_2	P_3	P_4
$\pm T_{subj}$ $-O$ . . .	Intran.	–	–	–
$\pm T_{actor}$ $\pm O$ . . .	–	Tran.	–	–
$\pm T_{agent}$ $\pm O$ . . .	–	–	SemTran.	–
$\pm T_{entity}$ $-O$ . . .	–	–	–	Equa.

(Pike 1962:234)

Like the cube, Pike's tetrahedron replaces the matrix so as to display a system with a greater number of features. Each of the four clause types, intransitive, transitive, semitransitive, and equational, is specified with respect to three features, T, O, and P. Each of the four faces of the pyramid represents a clause type: the clause type intransitive, for instance, is represented as

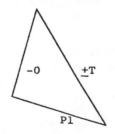

Thus each face of the figure constitutes the intersection of three features; its faces are to the
tetrahedron what cells are to the matrix.
      Alternatively, the finished theory suggested
by the matrix, though demanding a new sort of
representation, may not be representable by a figure. Pike's "matrix multiplication" (1962:230) is
an instance. In matrix multiplication, a matrix
is modified to display units as the intersection
of more than two features. The features that lie
along the two dimensions of the matrix are multiplied by a constant consisting of a "kernel matrix."
The whole is then the product of two matrices. It
is a sort of kangaroo figure: we could see it as

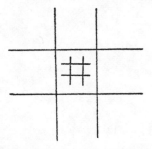

That it is a theoretical concept rather than a new
figure is indicated by Pike's formulating it not
graphically but mathematically. A multiplied
matrix,

I		A	B
		a b c	a b c
	1	x x x	x x x
	2	x x x	x x x
	3	x x x	x x x
II		a b c	a b c
	1	x x x	x x x
	2	x x x	x x x
	3	x x x	x x x

        (Pike 1962:227)

for instance, is expressed not as a figure but as
(228)

$$(1,2,3) \cdot (a,b,c) = M_k$$
$$(I,II) \cdot (A,B) \cdot M_k = M_z$$

Matrix multiplication remedies the characteristic inability of the matrix to handle a great
number of distinctions. A matrix represents a
unit as the intersection of two distinctive features; a cube or tetrahedron represents a unit as
the intersection of three distinctive features; a
multiplied matrix represents a unit as the intersection of a theoretically unlimited number of
distinctive features. The development of theory
that produces the tetrahedron and the multiplied
matrix, then, results from exploration of the neutral analogy furnished by the matrix figure. In
this case, the aspect of the model whose relevance
for the datum is under scrutiny is in the end
relegated to the negative analogy. This is the
fixing of the number of distinctive features at
two. It is built into the matrix figure; rele-
gating it to the negative analogy allows the
matrix to grow into the tetrahedron or to multiply
itself. More than the tetrahedron, the multiplied
matrix follows the logic of the matrix design, for
it is a matrix arrangement of matrices.
    An attempt to overcome the same limitation--
the fixing of the number of distinctions that can
simultaneously be made, at two--for the version of
the matrix figure that we have called the grid, is
to be found in the abstract lexical representation
of Chomsky and Halle (1968). In effect a modification of the figure, it combines the transformational grid, "in which the columns stand for the
successive units and the rows are labeled by the
names of the individual phonetic features," with
a set of phonological rules that alter that grid,
for each lexical item, "by deleting or adding
columns (units), by changing the specifications
assigned to particular rows (features) in partic-

ular columns, or by interchanging the positions of
columns" (296). The net result is a matrix in motion, in which columns come and go and change
places, and cells contain changeable information.
The phonological rules in the theory proposed by
Chomsky and Halle have the effect of making a
moving picture out of a series of "stills"--inter-
mediate phonological matrices--of the matrix. Such
a modification of the figure with an eye to getting
beyond the limitations of its two-dimensionality
thus has as well the virtue of overcoming the
static quality of the matrix figure in general,
relegated to the negative analogy by Austin,
Martinet, and Pfalz for diachronic theory. The
development of the neutral analogy presented by
the matrix figure here takes a different direction
from that proposed by Pike: in one case, the
fixed two-dimensionality of the model is supple-
mented by the notion of movement; in the other,
by the addition of a third dimension. Nevertheless, the matrix figure has in both cases proved
suggestive for the development of linguistic
theory; it has in both cases served the heuristic
function of models.
        It is for the development of transformational-
generative theory that the tree has been most suggestive. Its suggestiveness, unlike that of the
matrix, has two sources. One is of course the
figure itself; the other is the metaphor attaching
to the figure. Transformational theory shows
first of all the fruits of a literal interpretation of the tree figure. "Extraposition" of elements, for instance, alludes to what goes on in
the diagram;[12] so also do the various -fronting,
-raising, -spreading, -insertion, -attachment,
-placement, and -movement transformations[13]--all
named from the model-on-paper, from the operations
being performed on the diagram. The problem of
where to attach constituents in reordering transformations is a problem of diagramming, as are
other alterations in the tree that are necessi-
tated by the application of a transformation, over

and above the modification of the tree directly
wrought by that transformation--for example, node-
reduction (related to tree-pruning), and node-
relabelling. Various constraints on the application of transformations, as well, are formulated
in terms of the model-on-paper. Postal (1971), for
instance, discusses constraints on the movement of
NPs as what he terms "cross-over phenomena"--named
from what goes on in the figure: the reference is
to the movement of NP nodes across each other
along the horizontal dimension of the tree. Other
constraints exploit the vertical dimension of the
tree; "stacking," for instance, refers to the piling
up of like constituents (nodes) by self-embedding
(Stockwell, Schachter, and Partee 1973:442), as in
the configuration for relative clauses:

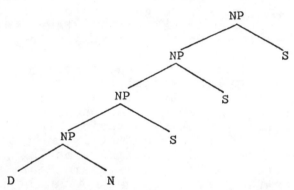

(Stockwell, Schachter, and Partee 1973:442)

Another example is Rosenbaum's "principle of minimum distance" (Stockwell, Schachter, and Partee,
532-536), itself the outgrowth of the "erasure
principle," the reference of which to the model-
on-paper is patent; the "principle of minimum
distance" exploits the vertical dimension of the
diagram by counting the number of branches in
the path between two nodes.
     Even the assumption that constituents are
ordered in deep structure may well be a response
to the exigencies of graphic representation: in

a two-dimensional medium, linearity is inherent.
Constrained to linear order, we choose left-to-
right because this is more natural in our culture,
although, as Weyl (1952:24-25) points out, "those
laws of which we can boast a reasonably certain
knowledge are invariant with respect to . . . the
interchange of left and right." Such terms as
"right-" and "left-branching" constructions also
reflect this constraint. (That it is a very real
constraint, attaching solely to the two-dimensionality of graphic representation, we shall see in
the next chapter.) Finally, the common miscon-
struction of the term "generative" as "productive"
is probably a product of the figure, which in
transformational-generative theory is always
upside-down and is naturally read from top to
bottom--from S down through intermediate constructions to a particular sentence, rather than from
the given sentence up through its analysis to its
characterization as an S.[14]
     With the tree as with the matrix, the response
to the fixed two-dimensionality of the figure has
been a development of transformational theory in
the direction of movement. As phonological rules
have the effect of making a moving picture out of
a series of "stills" of the matrix, so transformations have the effect of making a moving picture
out of a series of "stills"--intermediate phrase-
markers--of the tree. Again we have the notion
of rules as an attempt to overcome the limitations
of a two-dimensional model. The intermediate
phrase-markers which the addition of rules to the
grammar makes possible are related to each other
in sequence, as phases, so that the model then
requires that mutually exclusive representations
of the *explicandum*--for this is what different
stages in the derivation of a given sentence in
fact are--be held simultaneously in the mind.
(The dichotomy between deep and surface structure
itself, fundamental to transformational-generative
theory, makes the same demand: that two different
characterizations of the datum be considered

simultaneously.)   Augmenting the model by the
addition of rules, then, can be seen as an attempt
to get over into a third dimension; and the
elaboration of the concept of rule by the notion
of the transformational cycle appears in this
context as a further implementation of the concept
of movement, imposing, as it were, movement upon
movement, so that the rules that create a moving
picture of the tree are themselves in motion.
     Beyond such modifications of theory as these,
suggested by the exploration of the neutral analogy
presented by the figure itself, the model-on-paper,
are other modifications that proceed from the
metaphor attached to the figure.   Such components
of transformational-generative syntactic theory
as "embedding," "pruning," "chopping" and "grafting," preservation of the "root," substitution of
"vines" for trees--all are culled from the metaphor
of the tree.
     "Embedding" of sentences is postulated to
account for the phenomenon of recursion.   Its
metaphor is the grafting of a shoot--really a
tree in microcosm, after all.   Like Pike's
multiplied matrix, it is a sort of kangaroo
diagram:

It is replication according to the logic of the
figure.   We might call it a multiplied tree:
interpolation at a node is to the tree what
interpolation at a cell is to the matrix.
     "Pruning" (Ross 1969) is justifiable on
graphic grounds, it is true.   This configuration,

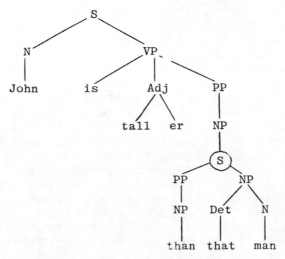

(Ross 1969:297)

in which a node S dominates a non-sentence, is
less elegant than this one:

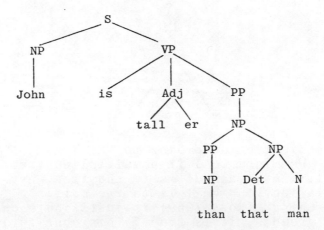

(Ross 1969:298)

But if the concept of pruning is based on graphic
considerations, its name comes from the metaphor.[15]
    So also "chopping" and "grafting" (Ross 1967).
Chopping is removing a construction or part of a
construction, which is then grafted onto the same
tree somewhere else.
    To the "root" of the tree corresponds the
initial S of a phrase structure tree diagram
(Emonds 1970)--its unique beginner. Here the
analogy is clearly with the metaphor rather than
the figure, inasmuch as the tree in transformational-generative grammar is upside-down, and can
hardly be considered to have its root at the top.
    A contrast to these notions, which merely add
to the theory as it stands, is the replacement of
trees by "vines" (Morin and O'Malley 1969). The
vine derives from the tree; but, unlike the tree,
it may--though it need not necessarily--be multi-
rooted. The following are all examples of vines:

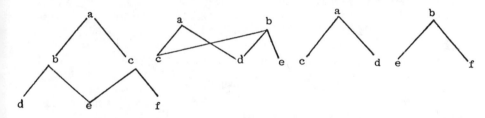

(Morin and O'Malley 1969:182)

A tree with more than one beginner, the vine is
offered as a better fit between the representation
and the thing represented. The sentence *I accuse
you of mailing the letter* (183), for example,
requires two disjoined trees,

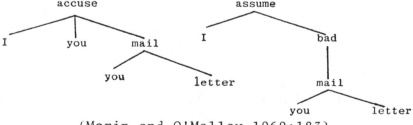

(Morin and O'Malley 1969:183)

but a single vine,

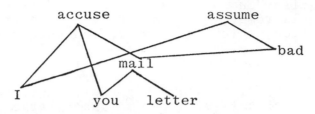

(Morin and O'Malley 1969:183)

It is at once a more compact structure and one
better suited to the representation of the datum:
for a single sentence, a single diagram. (In this
respect, the vine is to the tree what the tetrahedron is to the matrix, each being a more capacious model, accommodating a more complex datum in
a single diagram.) The figure has suggested its
own modification in the course of exploring the
neutral analogy. Like the limiting of features in
the matrix, the limiting of beginners in the tree
is relegated to the negative analogy; and with the
removal of this limitation, the tree, like the
matrix, gives way to a different figure.

     Nevertheless, vines, like roots, chopping
and grafting, and pruning, are named from the
metaphor of the tree. And who knows what further
elaboration of linguistic theory lies in that
metaphor? We shall look more closely, therefore,
at the process by which the metaphor is taken
literally: the exploration of the neutral analogy.
Graphic representation functions for a linguistic
theory as a model; in the case of the tree, the
model is attended by a metaphor. To the extent
that the metaphor replaces the figure as bearer of
the neutral analogy, it is a model once removed.
The encroaching realism that results from giving
prominence to the metaphor nearly equals that of
the diagram on the following page for the languages
of the world. This tree recalls Schleicher's
first version, which he later discarded, the *sich
verästelnde Baum*. The model that furnishes the

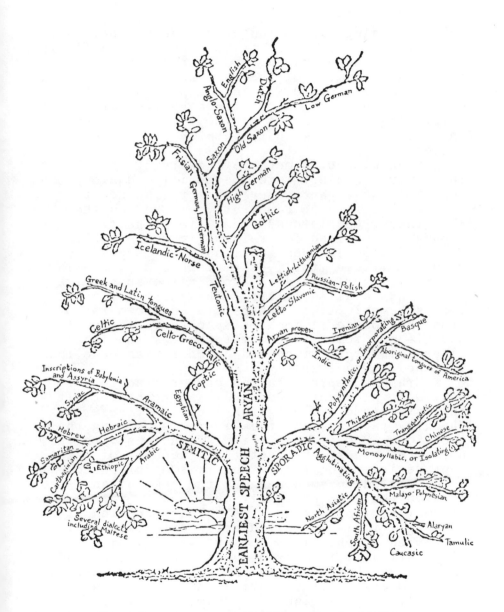

(Von Ostermann and Giegengack 1936)

neutral analogy is no longer a figure, no longer
schematic; it is a real tree. Replacing a figure
with its metaphor may not in itself lead to unwarranted development of theory. But if the neutral
analogy as it unfolds is then assigned all to the
positive analogy, none to the negative, it is not
surprising that aspects of the resulting theory
have little to do with the *explicandum*, English
sentences.

     Even without a metaphor, carrying off all of
the neutral analogy into the positive analogy can
result in unwarranted development. We see this in
such aspects of the comparative method as the
abruptness, completeness, and simultaneity of
separation posited for related languages (Bloomfield 1933:318); these notions seem to proceed
from the figure itself, the graphic design. Thus
all Schleicher's care to avoid a too-suggestive
figure has availed little. The substitution of a
more schematic tree perhaps stayed the metaphor
from the course it took in synchronic linguistics;
but, if so, removing the metaphor as the object of
literal interpretation did no more than make room
for the figure itself.

     Graphic representation cannot lead to war-
ranted development, then, unless the notions it
suggests are checked against the *explicandum*.
Checking them against the figure is begging the
question. But even if this is done, as with the
notion of vines, the fact that the name of a concept derives from the metaphor is unfortunate.
Once settled on such a name, the temptation is to
develop the concept itself on grounds, not of
grammar, but of botany. Or take the notion of
pruning: it is justified metaphorically; it is
justified graphically; but unless it is justified
linguistically, the bridge between analogue and
explicandum has not been built. This is what it
means to explore the neutral analogy offered by
a model. A good figure has a wild civility; it
cannot otherwise be suggestive; the problem is to
keep its suggestiveness within bounds. Thus, for

the tree, Darwin at the outset (1859:116-130) care-
fully charts the elements both of metaphor and of
design. Each graphic element--node, branch, and so
on--is accorded a meaning, to which limits are set.
For scientific theory requires a model with room
to grow in, but not without all semblance of fit.

    Because a figure is assumed to have been tai-
lored to its theory, the dangers of model-making
are greater if the analogue is graphic representation. Martinet warns (personal communication) that
a diagram is likely to "harden" the pattern represented, though actually parts of it are "softer"
than others; that the compulsion is strong to let
representation replace reality. The result is a
random harvest of notions like vines and roots, a
perhaps harmlessly bizarre nomenclature that nevertheless interposes itself between theory and *explicandum*.[16] Because a figure *can* be tailored to its
theory, what we have said about graphic representation has consequences for its design. We have
considered linguistic theory as a product of
graphic representation; now we shall consider
graphic representation as a product of linguistic
theory.

Graphic representation and
graphic design

If, as its effect on the development of linguistic theory indicates, graphic representation
furnishes the models for linguistic science, we
must now ask how it does so. How does a diagram
serve as the analogue for a linguistic *explicandum*?
How does it provide the neutral analogy whose exploration leads to the modification of linguistic
theory? To answer such questions we must inquire
into the nature of graphic representation, taking
the second of our two perspectives, the principles
of graphic design.

Graphic representation
and the principles of graphic design

Graphic representation is a language, and the
principles of graphic design are its grammar. Because figures are made to stand for something else,
however, the relationship between form and meaning
is more complicated than it is for natural languages. Graphic representation is in fact more
like a code than like natural language; for it
bears at once its own meaning--its meaning as an
utterance in a language--and the meaning grafted
on it by its use as a symbol--its meaning as an
utterance in a code. We shall call the two kinds
of meaning "visual meaning" and "symbolic meaning."
But there is still another aspect of the meaning
of a figure, what might be called its connotation,

as opposed to the first two kinds of meaning, which
are its denotation. For just as an utterance in a
natural language carries expressive overtones not
governed by its denotation--harmonics, as it were,
of the note sounded by its denotation--so a figure
carries expressive value. This we shall call
"expressive meaning."

Visual meaning

     Like any language, graphic representation has
a vocabulary and a grammar. The vocabulary of
graphic representation is the "art elements."[17]
Some of them must be ruled out for linguistics
on grounds of impracticability; thus, from the
complete inventory of art elements,

line	value	texture
shape	hue	volume
space	intensity	movement

The last two, volume and movement, must be delet-
ed: volume, because graphic representation is not
plastic; movement, because it is not dynamic.
Three more are ruled out on grounds of impracti-
cality: texture, hue, and intensity are difficult
and expensive to reproduce. The four remaining
art elements--line, shape, space, value--are the
vocabulary of graphic representation for linguistics. Though they are not wholly independent of
each other, they enjoy a limited autonomy. There
is line, an independent element in which value
(relative lightness or darkness) may or may not
be significant. There is shape, in which value
may or may not be significant, but which surely
depends on line for its realization. And there
is space--two-dimensional for our purposes--
against which the presence of line and shape
contrasts with their absence.
     Klee sees the relationship between line and
shape as more complex. He distinguishes three
"characters" (1961:115):

"linear character" (linear-active, planar-passive):

"middle character" ("neither line nor plane" [109]):

"planar character" (linear-passive, planar-active):

Configurations of a middle character are the ones we shall have most to do with. For these, Klee gives three "basic forms," each of which may be construed in two ways (32):

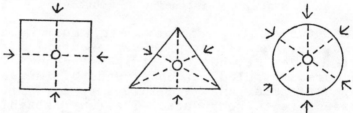

"discharge of tension from outside or subtractive"

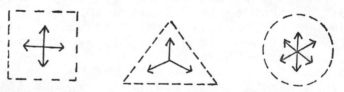

"discharge of tension from within or additive"

There are, then, things a particular shape can be made to say, and things it cannot; and things it *will* say, despite the designer's intentions to the contrary.

The four art elements are manipulated according to the grammar of graphic representation, the
principles of composition. Different treatments
of the subject list different principles.[18] There
are three, however, that are indispensable: balance,
rhythm, and emphasis.

Balance is of two sorts, overt and "occult"
(Scott 1951:43-46). Overt or "static" balance
(Kepes 1944:36) comprises "axial balance" and
"radial balance" (Scott, 43-45). Axial balance
corresponds to Weyl's (1952) bilateral symmetry;
radial balance is his cyclic symmetry, the symmetry of snowflakes and rose windows. In overt
balance, like things balance each other along axes
or around a focal point; occult or "dynamic" balance, in contrast, is the product of elements that
are, not like, but unlike--"a pound of iron balan-
cing a pound of feathers" (Kepes, 36). The numer-
ous ways in which occult balance is achieved all
involve compensation. The art elements compensate
one for another: a small dark shape, for instance,
balances a large light one. It is easy to see
that occult balance has tension, dynamism, a sort
of centrifugal force; it will suit some meanings
and not others. We can sum up the various kinds
of balance as

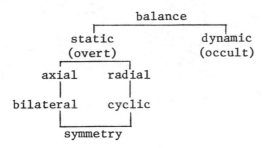

Rhythm--the second design principle--is, in
a word, repetition: it is *"expected* recurrence"
(Scott, 63). It corresponds to Weyl's translatory
symmetry, the symmetry of frieze designs,

(Weyl 1952:49)

and centipedes:

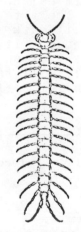

(Weyl 1952:5)

There are several kinds of rhythm (Scott, 63-65)
besides repetition of the same unit or interval:
progression of identical shapes of increasing or
decreasing size; alternation of dissimilar units;
and occult rhythm, the repetition of "whole systems of relationships." Simple repetition creates
what Klee (1961:230-231) calls "dividual" struc-

tures, like the cellular structure of a flower.
Progression, alternation, and occult rhythm create
"individual" structures, like the flower itself.
Addition or subtraction of a unit leaves a dividual
structure unchanged, but turns an individual structure into a new form (Klee, 257). We can sum up
the various kinds of rhythm as

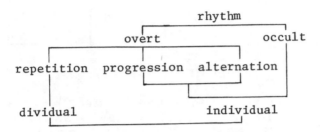

     The third design principle is emphasis. The
means by which emphasis, overt or occult, is
achieved are infinitely various; but always, as
balance depends on compensation and rhythm depends
on repetition, emphasis depends on contrast. Part
of a design may be darker (or lighter) than the
rest; or larger (or smaller); or its position may
give it emphasis. The focal point of a design
with overt balance is naturally the center, just
as the last word in a sentence naturally receives
emphasis. The focal point of a design with occult
balance is created by the arrangement of elements
within that design, as the first word of a sentence is given emphasis by inverting word order.
     The vocabulary of graphic representation,
then, comprises the art elements of line, shape,
space, and value. The grammar of graphic repre-
sentation--the arrangement of these elements--
follows the design principles: balance, rhythm,
and emphasis. But we have not accounted for all
the ways in which a figure makes a meaningful
statement. So far we have been looking at part
of the meaning of graphic representation, what we
have called visual meaning. In reality, of course,
visual meaning is inextricable from expressive

and symbolic meaning. Nevertheless, the existence
of visual meaning is demonstrated by the possibility of visual ambiguity.   The right-hand figure
in each of the following pairs is visually ambiguous:

(Arnheim 1964:9-11)

We cannot read the right-hand figures with any
certainty: are they meant to have the assym-
metrical proportions of the figures on the left
in each pair?--or are they intended as symmetrical:

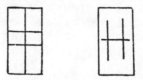

By their visual meaning, figures make a statement that we can weigh, doubt, argue about,
without appealing to anything outside the figures
themselves: we do not need to ask what they
stand for.

Expressive meaning

     Expressive meaning resides in the "expres-
sive value" (Watkins 1946:10) of the art elements
out of which the message is constructed, and the
connotations accruing from the culture in which
sender and receiver participate. The expressive
value of line (Watkins, 10) is:

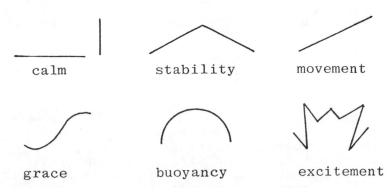

calm   stability   movement

grace   buoyancy   excitement

The symbols get their expressive value from their
function as a "simplification, or graphic shorthand" for the natural world (11). Cultural connotations are likely to echo expressive value: connotations of eternity adhere to the circle from
the mandala in Oriental religion; other connotations adhere to the tree in western culture from
the Tree of Knowledge and the Cross.

Expressive and cultural associations are
communicated by a design independently of its subject matter (Anderson, 60). The expressive meaning of the circle, for instance,

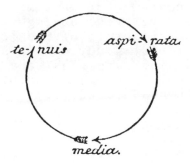

(Schleicher 1888:97)

is eminently suited to an eternally repeated process. It is the expressive meaning of a design,
moreover, that furnishes metaphor; if the expressive meaning takes over the figure, unwarranted

development of theory can result, as with the tree
in synchronic linguistics.

Symbolic meaning

     The symbolic meaning of a design is its
meaning, its effectiveness as a symbol. A figure must reconcile its intended meaning, its
subject matter, with the visual and expressive
meaning of its design; their congruence is the
measure of a good design. It is a question of
translation. Like a good translation, a good
representation is isomorphic with its subject
matter: in it, as Y. R. Chao puts it, "symbol
complexes [are] in *iconic relations* with object
complexes" (1968:221).[19] We shall call such a
figure an isomorph. The idea is not new. Bell
(1867:35) gives it as "the fundamental principle
of Visible Speech that all Relations of Sound
are symbolized by Relations of Form." We have
arrived again, by a different route, at the
question of whether graphic representation
occupies in linguistic theory the place of models
in scientific theory. For what is the conception
of the model as a material analogue but a
statement of the principle of iconic relations?
Indeed, Chao's (1962) study of the senses of
the term "model" indicates that the one element
common to them all is "some structural similarity
shared by two things" (1968:202).
     An isomorph, Chao takes pains to point out,
is to be distinguished from an icon. The former
is the "relevance of the structure of symbol
complexes to the structure of objects"; the
latter, the "fortuitous relevance between a
simple symbol and its object" (1968:220). Many
road signs are icons. The symbols > and <, in
both mathematics and linguistics, are icons.
The Chinese box diagram is an icon, in that it
"clearly indicates·the notion of constructions

being nested" (Gleason 1965:158). It is at the
same time an isomorph insofar as it represents
similar relations by similar means, so that it
recapitulates the structure of the *explicandum*.
     Chao dismisses iconic symbols as essentially
unimportant, and no doubt they are a luxury;
nevertheless, for a theory of graphic representation in linguistics, iconicity is as important
as isomorphism. Its importance is negative.
Isomorphism characterizes a figure that will
be fruitful for theory--that furnishes a neutral
analogy at least some aspects of which will
ultimately be part of the positive analogy.
Conversely, negative analogy is to be shunned.
Thus what Chao (1968:219) calls "irrelevant
iconic features" loom large. As taking the
metaphor literally is a sort of imperialism
of expressive meaning, so taking the figure
literally is a sort of imperialism of visual
meaning. Visual meaning, the figure as a design,
usurps the place of symbolic meaning; iconicity
supplants isomorphism. The result, as we saw
for the tree, can be the unwarranted development
of theory.
     Our theory of graphic representation for
linguistics, then, comprises the aspects of
graphic design set out in the chart on the
following page.

VISUAL MEANING

  art elements

        line, space, shape, value

  design principles

    balance . . . . compensation

```
                  ┌──────────┐
               overt          occult
            ┌────┴────┐
          axial     radial
            │          │
        bilateral   cyclic
            └─────┬────┘
               symmetry
```

    rhythm . . . . repetition

```
                    ┌────────────────┐
                 overt              occult
        ┌─────────┬────────┬───────────┐
   repetition  progression  alternation
        │              ┌──────┴──────┐
     dividual              individual
        └──────────────────────┘
```

    emphasis . . . . contrast

EXPRESSIVE MEANING

        expressive value
        cultural connotations

SYMBOLIC MEANING

```
        isomorph────────────────icon
            │                     │
      material analogy    irrelevant iconic features
```

*The design of graphic representation
for linguistics*

Now let us see what our theory of graphic
representation can do to unravel the tangle of
correspondences between form and meaning that
exists for graphic representation in linguistics:

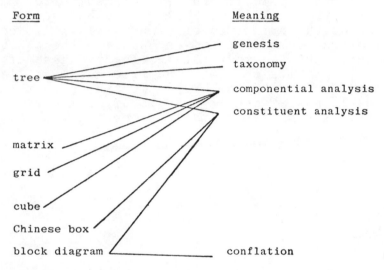

What we would like to do is remove the synonymy
and homonymy--the knots, as it were, that occur
at the points marked "tree," "componential analysis," and "block diagram." We shall not take the
Gordian way out, but rather use our theory of
graphic representation as a principled basis for
the unraveling.

At the same time, we shall be looking at
graphic representation from the other of our two
perspectives, as a component of linguistic science. Indeed, we cannot avoid doing so: for the
aspect of the meaning of a figure that we have
called symbolic meaning--which presumes the relationship of material analogy between the figure
and something else--is the very aspect of its
meaning by virtue of which we can speak of graphic

design at all. "Design" implies a match between
figure and meaning, as "scientific model" implies
a match between analogue and *explicandum*.

The tree design

Line and space are the art elements from
which the tree design is built. Its balance,
insofar as the principle of binarity is followed,
is bilateral symmetry; its emphasis is the unique
beginner. But the most interesting thing about
the design is its rhythm. The tree has what Klee
calls individual rhythm. This is true even though
it clearly has a sort of translatory symmetry--
that is, it replicates itself along the vertical
axis:

Because a tree has a top and bottom, and often a
left and right as well, adding to it or sub-
tracting from it changes it. Even rearranging
it makes the figure take on a different shape:

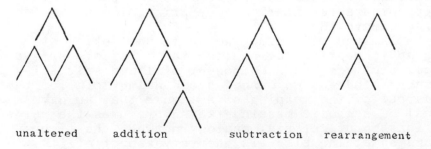

unaltered   addition   subtraction   rearrangement

The tree is therefore peculiarly suited to
representation of things having an inherent order
or hierarchy of some sort. The repetition of
units--of the combination of node and branch--is
more than simple addition; in the tree, repetition
is recursion. Such stubbornly asymmetrical (in
the mathematical sense) notions as genesis, taxonomy, constituent analysis--all are reflected in
the individual rhythm of the tree; for one cannot
subtract from, add to, or rearrange the units of
such systems without toppling the whole structure.
The tree design captures the intransigence of time
and space.
    The tree is as unsuited to componential anal-
ysis as it is suited to the other three meanings.
A key--a tree for componential analysis--is characterized by the interchangeability of rows; but
we have seen that rearrangement of units is counter to individual rhythm. A key is characterized
by overlapping classes; but we have seen that a
symmetrical relationship among units is counter
to individual rhythm. A key is characterized by
items all of equal rank (all nodes are features,
all terminal elements are sounds); but we have
seen that equality of units is counter to individual rhythm. The characteristics of a key are in
fact just the characteristics of dividual rhythm.
A dividual structure, then, is the kind of design
we should look for to express componential analysis, and not the tree at all.
    Eliminating componential analysis from the
list of meanings for the tree, however, still
leaves us with homonymy. We have already discussed the problems presented by the tree design
for the other three meanings. For taxonomy,
there is the problem of overlapping classes: in
linguistic taxonomies, some overlap seems to be
inevitable. But this we can solve by the use of
"Rorschach" diagrams like the one of Pike's reproduced in Chapter 2 and the ones for symmetry and
rhythm given in this chapter. For genesis, however, there is the problem of the visual meaning

of the tree; as we have said, the limitations of
the comparative method--abrupt and simultaneous
separation of daughter languages from the parent
and from each other--are largely the limitations
of the figure. For constituent analysis, there is
the problem not only of the influence of the figure on the development of grammatical theory (such
notions as extraposition, ordered elements in the
deep structure, and so on), but also of the influence of its metaphor (such notions as pruning,
chopping and grafting, and so on); that is, both
the visual meaning and the expressive meaning of
the tree design have furnished a neutral analogy
that ended in the unwarranted development of
linguistic theory.

One proposal for circumventing the limita-
tions of the tree for historical linguistics is
Southworth's amalgam of tree and wave diagrams
(Southworth 1964; quoted in Anttila 1972:308-309).
A wave diagram allows the representation of over-
lapping relationships--the point of Schmidt's
Wellentheorie--not expressed in a tree:

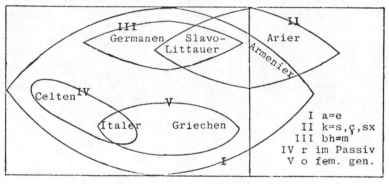

(Schrader 1883:99)

But it cannot replace the tree. The tree, in
Southworth's words (558), "shows splitting processes but cannot show overlapping relationships,
whereas an isogloss map shows all the relationships at one particular stage of the history, but

cannot show more than one stage."   Southworth's
object is a new design that gives "a truer and
clearer picture of linguistic history" (557). The
amalgam (actually its penultimate version, but the
best one) looks like this:

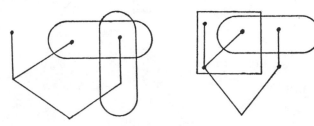

(Southworth 1964:562)

The wave component, in rectangles, expresses time
only indirectly, by length along the vertical axis
of the tree: the longer the rectangle, the earlier
the phenomenon occurred.   The wave component
largely takes over representation of *Nebeneinander*;
the tree component represents *Nacheinander*.
     If the construction is unwieldy enough to
limit its usefulness and to prevent its substitution for tree diagrams with the genetic meaning,
it is not the underlying theory that makes it so.
On the contrary, it is legitimate, and certainly
not unprecedented, to combine different models for
a single *explicandum* provided they are complemen-
tary--the wave and particle models in physics, for
instance (Hesse 1966:53; Toulmin 1953:35). Now,
Schleicher's and Schmidt's versions of linguistic
history, as Leskien first pointed out (Anttila
1972:307), are complementary. It is reasonable to
assume that the two figures are also complementary.
Perhaps the problem is one of design? "Bilder,"
Schmidt himself said (1872:28), "haben in der
wissenschaft nur ser geringen wert."   Indeed, it
is hard to imagine Southworth's figure representing, say, all the isoglosses for Indo-European.
It is harder still to imagine it showing the
particularity of Hockett's "detail" from a wave
diagram for the Germanic languages,

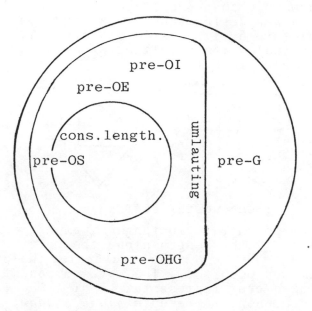

(Hockett 1958:69)

        Let us see what our theory of graphic repre-
sentation has to say about it. What are the art
elements of which the design is constructed? No
sooner is the question asked, than we have found
the problem: a single element is employed in
addition to space, and that is line. The rectan-
gular shapes are simply line configurations, forms
of what Klee calls a middle character; the nodes
are simply points on a line. Clearly this is
overburdening a single graphic device. We have
met this problem before, and shall meet it again.
Most of the figures used in linguistics, all of
which are two-dimensional, are constructed from
line and space. The vocabulary of graphic representation was limited at the outset to four of
the art elements: line, space, shape, value. Now
we find it has shrunk to two. Though our theory
has failed to provide an answer to these difficulties, it *has* provided the questions.

Visual meaning is as troublesome for IC
representation in general as it is for tree diagrams with the meaning of constituent analysis.
Attempts to better the match between figure and
explicandum like those that follow all address
themselves to the same problem and use the same
means.

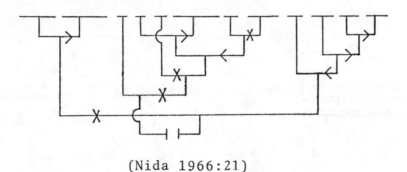

(Nida 1966:21)

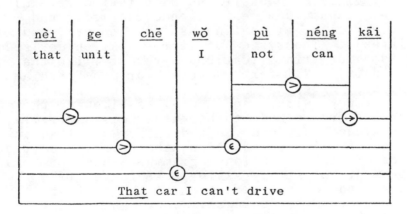

(Hockett 1958:247)

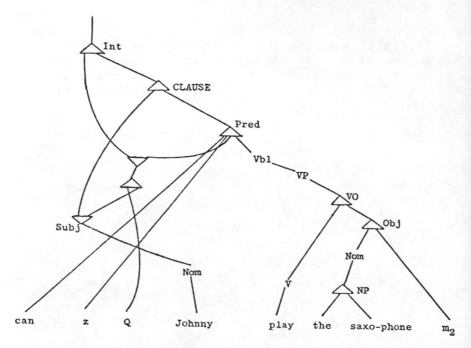

(Lamb 1966:25)

The diagrams of Hockett and Nida introduce additional graphic devices for endocentricity and
exocentricity, discontinuous constituents, and
parataxis. The system of representation devised
by Lamb for stratificational grammar (like that
of Hudson [1971] for "systemic" or neo-Firthian
grammar) solves the problem of discontinuous
constituents with graphic devices allowing the
branches from a node to be either disjunctively
or conjunctively ordered and either simultaneous
or sequential. In addition, the greatly modified
trees of stratificational grammar--when they
represent not simply a single sentence, like the
diagram above, but a section of the grammar--
incorporate other changes. They can be bidirec-
tional, somewhat in the way of the double tree
from Pike reproduced in Chapter 1; and they can
have more than one beginner, somewhat in the way

of Morin and O'Malley's vines, at points where
the "knot pattern" combines input from two
sources, the "alternation" and "tactic" patterns:

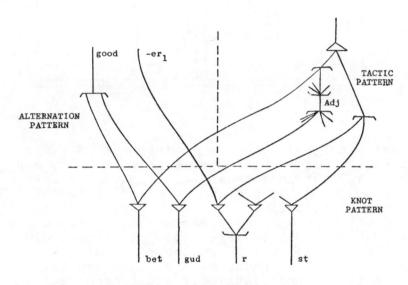

(Lamb 1966:17)

Essentially, the problems dealt with by the
modifications of Nida, Hockett, and Lamb are all
different faces of the same thing. This is at
the root, as well, of the difficulties presented
by the influence of the tree figure on the development of transformational-generative grammar.
It is the linearity of graphic representation.
That it is a defect of graphic representation in
general rather than the tree diagram in particular
is supported by the fact that other kinds of IC
representation contrive devices to circumvent
the same limitations; for instance, Francis
modifies the Chinese box to represent endocentricity and exocentricity:

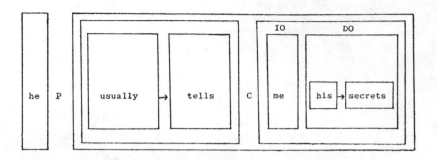

(Francis 1958:313)

Linearity not only imposes an inescapable order
on constituents, but also entails continuity and
hypotaxis. For in a chain, contiguous elements
are necessarily connected, and noncontiguous
elements necessarily unconnected; and only the
introduction of special symbols can, by an act of
representation, as it were, abrogate these relationships. Adjacency or enclosure within the
same block or box cannot mean at once hypotaxis
and parataxis, endocentricity and exocentricity,
membership in the same construction and membership (because of a discontinuous construction
intervening) in two different constructions.
Special symbols are required as long as representation is two-dimensional.

Expressive meaning also presents difficulties
for the tree. As we have seen, it furnishes the
diagram with a metaphor which at times usurps the
place of the analogue.

Commending Reed-Kellogg diagrams is rather
like commending the English writing system,
orthography's ugly duckling; but for the representation of constituent analysis, old-fashioned
Reed-Kellogg diagrams might well be the best we
can do. For one thing, the Reed-Kellogg system
is more commodious than any we have looked at.

As Gleason (1965:142-151) points out, it covers
everything from

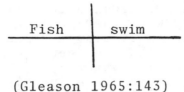

(Gleason 1965:143)

to

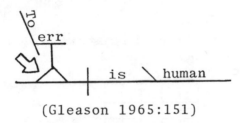

(Gleason 1965:151)

If line and space are the only art elements
pressed into service for graphic representation
in linguistics, Reed-Kellogg notation at least
exploits them to the fullest. More than that,
Reed-Kellogg diagrams have several things to
recommend them. First, the figure is neither a
tree nor a block diagram (though it has elements
of both), and so does not participate in homonymy.
Second, it represents simultaneously both surface
structure and deep structure, something none of
the other figures we have considered does: any
constituent perched on a sort of two-legged stand
is an embedded sentence (though the converse does
not hold). The other IC representations show
either surface structure or deep structure, but
not both at the same time. Finally, and perhaps
most important, Reed-Kellogg diagrams support no
metaphor, neither fauna nor flora.
        It is true that Reed-Kellogg diagrams, like
the others, are cumbersome, heavy with the weight
of auxiliary notation, special symbols and the
like; for they too cannot represent discontinuity;

they too are subject to the constraint of
linearity built into graphic representation. Like
Southworth's proposed modification of the tree
for historical linguistics, Reed-Kellogg diagrams
lose in simplicity what they gain in accuracy. We
have not succeeded in finding a replacement for
tree diagrams for either the genetic meaning or
the meaning of constituent analysis; and it is
beginning to look as if the exigencies of a two-
dimensional medium are insurmountable.

The matrix design

A design very like the matrix,

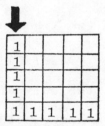

(Klee 1961:217)

is characterized by Klee (1961:217) as "the most
primitive structural rhythm"; it is, he says, no
more than "a combination of the two directions,"
"an addition of units in two dimensions." It is
in many ways the direct opposite of the tree
design.
     The meaning of the matrix figure lies in its
dividual rhythm. Klee might have said, the relent-
less addition of units; for this, as we have seen,
is what makes the figure. It gives it its characteristic balance, its translatory symmetry: the
matrix is translatory in both directions, horizontally and vertically, outdoing in this respect even
the centipede, which is translatory in one direction only. The absolute likeness of each cell to
every other comes from translatory symmetry--and
a fearful symmetry it is, since it appears to

determine the figure's great negotiability. The
matrix is expandable; it is modular; it is the
blueprint for its own expansion. But so is the
tree; and we have noted the coincidence of war-
ranted extension with the matrix and unwarranted
extension with the tree. How do the designs
differ? Repetition of units in the matrix is the
simplest sort of propagation, addition. Repetition
of units in the tree is recursion, a complicated
sort of propagation which locates each successive
repetition within an unfolding hierarchic structure. Repeating a system of relationships (the
configuration of node and branch), like building
a house of cards, precludes a democratic interchangeability of units. Conversely, repeating
identical units (cells) leaves no room for the
expression of hierarchy.

So it is that the tree design with its individual rhythm is not suited to the representation
of interchangeable units, but the matrix design
with its dividual rhythm is made for it. We have
called the cells of the matrix the product or
intersection of the two dimensions; we might
instead have called them the overlapping of two
classes, since every cell is a point at which two
criteria overlap. In this the matrix is diamet-
rically opposed to the tree; for not only taxonomic trees, but trees of any sort, are ill-formed
if they represent the intersection of classes.
Therefore the notion,

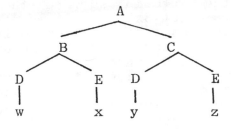

is better put as

	B	C
D	w	y
E	x	z

--not as a tree but as a matrix (Kay 1969:81; Pike
1962:230-231; Wallace and Atkins 1960:409). Representing it by a tree entails the extension of the
theme of constituent analysis to a concept that
falls within the other great theme of componential analysis: it entails the collision of two
opposite theories.
     The dividual rhythm of the matrix design
gives it its characteristic emphasis as well. What
fills the cells is the marrow of the figure. It is
for this reason that the grid deploys the elements
of componential analysis less than strategically.
In the grid, the arrangement of elements--sounds,
features, feature specifications--is at odds with
the figure's emphasis. What fills the cells is a
collection of uninterpretable symbols (+, -, O)--
uninterpretable until decoded by recourse to the
elements on the perimeter.
     The extreme simplicity of the matrix design
leaves it without expressive meaning. It is, after
all, no more than the juxtaposition of the two
dimensions of the pictorial surface--the bare bones
of graphic representation. Yet it is perhaps its
very inexpressiveness that has endowed it with a
heuristic usefulness for linguistic theory. Its
static quality, for instance--for unlike the tree,
it has no built-in directionality--is what suggested the theories of Pfalz, Austin, and Martinet,
the notion of sound change as movement. Certainly
its simplicity facilitated its extension--and the
concomitant extension of componential analysis--
to different kinds of linguistic *explicanda*. At

any rate, it has not proved the fertile ground
for the growth of metaphor that the tree has been.
      The matrix design gives iconic features al-
most as little play. Putting outside the matrix
units that stand outside the system (as in the
figure from Trubetzkoy) uses the matrix as an
icon; so does letting the order of columns follow
the oral cavity, so that left to right reflects
front to back. And matrix arrangements of vowels
tend to turn into schematic representations of
the oral cavity. Thus

i	u
e	o
ɛ	ɔ
æ	a

can transform itself into

```
        i              u

      e              o

        ɛ        ɔ
           æ
              a
```

with chameleon rapidity. On the whole, however,
symbolic meaning does not present problems for
the matrix design.

The box design

      The cube and the matrix are synonyms; but
they are also complementary. The cube accommodates three features; the matrix, two. Thus we

shall not be concerned to eliminate synonymy, but,
if we can, to exploit it.
      Potentially misleading elements of visual
meaning for the cube are its rhythm and its emphasis. The matrix has dividual rhythm; the cube has
individual rhythm. It exhibits occult repetition,
as the trouble we had resolving it into six occur-
rences of a single shape testifies. We could prize
it apart only by using a special tool, the concept
of projection to different planes, thus setting
the figure apart from all the others. The difference between the cube and other figures makes
it hard to see the cube as the logical extension
of the matrix, as simply a more capacious matrix.
This becomes clearer when we consider extending it
one feature further. Where can the figure go? We
can of course resort to graphic representation of
four-dimensional constructions, like this one:

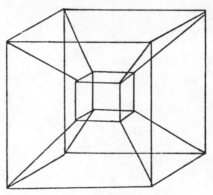

(Lotz 1967:3)

But representation of a four-dimensional figure
in a two-dimensional medium makes a configuration
almost impossible to read; and this is compounded
by the fact that, like all the other figures, it
is built out of only two art elements, line and
space. Moreover, where is the figure to go from
here? What about five features? Six?
      The problem of the figure's emphasis is part
of the larger problem of its rhythm.   Though

componential analysis is a dividual concept, the
cube is an individual structure. The front of the
cube is the focal point, because it is the only
side seen clearly and non-obliquely (the back, not
seen obliquely, is nevertheless obscured). Whatever is placed at the front of the figure receives
emphasis; thus, though the cube does not, like the
tree, impose a hierarchical arrangement on the
data, it does throw part of the data into relief--
generally undesirable for the expression of componential analysis.
    Perhaps the most interesting aspect of the
difficulties presented by the visual meaning of
the cube is its ambiguity. Because only the two
art elements, line and space, construct the figure,
the cube, like the examples of pure design we
looked at earlier, is visually ambiguous. The cube
may easily dissolve into a collection of points
joined by lines, as a slight distortion makes
clear:

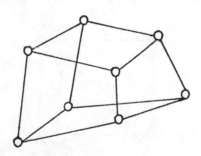

The figure wavers between two- and three-dimensionality: it may be read as a seine-like
structure, when it is intended as a structure of
slab-like pieces. The consequence for its symbolic meaning is that the componential analysis
is carried by the lines between the points (properly speaking, the corners); whereas actually,
as we noted, the sides of the construction carry
the analysis. That cube diagrams are nonetheless
intended to be read differently from network diagrams is clear from a comparison of the two.
Jakobson's cube diagram for the componential

analysis of Russian declension, for instance,

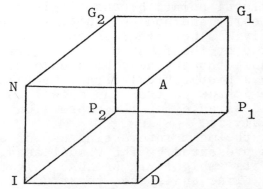

(Jakobson 1963:149
[Roman letters replace Cyrillic])

looks very different from a network diagram for
the same thing:

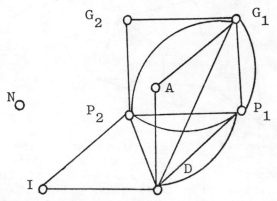

This network version of the same componential
analysis rests on point and line: points represent the units of the system, the cases; lines
represent shared features.

Value used together with line transforms
the cube into an unambiguously three-dimensional
configuration,

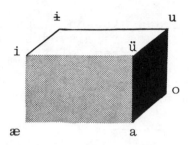

but destroys its transparency and with it the
armature of three-feature analysis. Forchhammer's
early version of the cube, probably the prototype,
uses line rather than value to effect unambiguous
three-dimensionality:

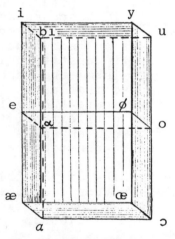

(Forchhammer 1924:42)

This preserves its transparency, but leaves the
same problem as did the modifications proposed for
IC representation--too great a burden on the
single art element of line.
      The expressive meaning of the cube poses no
problem; nor does it, like the tree, carry a metaphor. As for its symbolic meaning, the iconicity
of the cube is often squandered. In the cube

diagrams of Hockett and Gleason, reproduced in
Chapter 3, what a chance is missed by not putting
the front vowels at the front of the figure, the
back vowels at the back!
    The second sort of box diagram, the Chinese
box, has static balance and radial symmetry, like
Klee's figure,

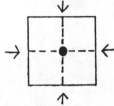

It consists in the repetition of a single shape of
what Klee calls a middle character. With the tree-
like scaffolding of all IC representation, the
Chinese box, like other figures for the meaning of
constituent analysis, is an individual structure.
This is because its overt repetition is not simple
repetition, but progression: the repeated squares
are graduated in size, so that as one reads out
from the center of the figure they get larger and
less specific. The concentricity of the repeated
shapes creates the figure's emphasis. Its focal
point is the center of concentric rectangles, the
core of the figure.
    The expressive meaning of the Chinese box
includes its likeness to Venn diagrams, a tool in
the algebra of sets and symbolic logic for the
expression of inclusion relations:

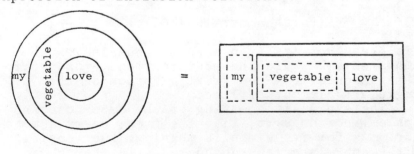

Both express the implication: love ———► vegetable
———► my; reverse this, and bending the arrows of
implication a little gives an endocentric construction:

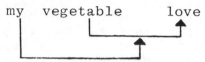

Here, then, expressive meaning reinforces visual
meaning, and the concentricity of the figure is
thus a formidable obstacle.
    As for its symbolic meaning, the concentricity
of repeated rectangles, which creates the figure's
emphasis, makes expression of endocentricity
(Hockett 1958:189) and exocentricity inherent in
the Chinese box. A construction's endocentricity
is automatically entailed by the diagram,

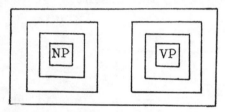

just as constituent function ([NP,S] [NP,VP] and
so on) is automatically entailed by tree diagrams.
This has its drawbacks: even so simple a
construction as

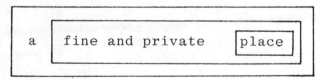

is at odds with the insistent singular emphasis
of the figure.
    Finally, let us look at the block diagram,
the last of our three kinds of box diagrams.
Though it can be isomorphic with either a tree
or a matrix, the block diagram is better suited

to the meaning of conflation than to that of constituent analysis: its symbolic meaning is a
conflated matrix by virtue of the fact that its
visual meaning is a conflated matrix. Its visual
meaning is a conflated matrix through converting
a dividual structure into an individual structure.
The underlying matrix expressing a full system has
dividual, overt rhythm; conflation, erasing some
of the boundaries between cells, converts this to
individual, occult rhythm--a rhythm literally
obscured. Clearly, the block diagram for the
meaning of conflation serves Chao's principle of
iconic relations. The figure preserves the matrix
in all respects save those which have altered with
time or from system to system, and whose alteration is the subject of the figure's statement.
     We have unsnarled the correspondences between
form and meaning to some extent:

Form   Meaning

double tree _____ taxonomy

                                        genesis
tree -<
                                        constituent analysis

matrix _____ componential analysis

block diagram _____ conflation

We have done so by means of several deletions: the
grid, because it is an ineffective use of the matrix design; the key--the tree for componential
analysis--because the tree design is an irreme-
diably bad fit for this meaning; the cube, because
it is an individual structure used for a dividual
concept; the Chinese box, because the neutral
analogy it furnishes is likely to be misleading;
the block diagram for constituent analysis, because the figure is a better fit for the meaning
of conflation. We have made only one addition,
the double tree for taxonomy.

This revision is unsatisfactory. For one
thing, the tree is still a homonym: neither
Southworth's proposed figure for the genetic
meaning nor Reed-Kellogg notation for the meaning
of constituent analysis is a good replacement for
the tree. For another, the problems we noted for
the neutral analogy presented by both the tree and
the matrix remain unresolved. And finally, the
exigencies of graphic representation--two-dimen-
sionality and the scant vocabulary of art elements--
are still a problem. In fact, what is needed is
not fewer figures, but more.

New directions for models
in linguistic theory

We have taken two approaches to graphic
representation in linguistics: the philosophy of
science, and the principles of graphic design; now,
the two perspectives converge. We began the discussion of graphic representation in linguistics
by looking at the three kinds of figures that are
currently used, three graphic least common denom-
inators. This inevitably imposed a taxonomy of
graphic representation in linguistics, and it then
became possible to see the homonymy and synonymy
that hold between figures and analytic techniques.
When we considered as well the evidence that
graphic representation functions as a model for
linguistic science, the problem it presents for
the development of linguistic theory became apparent. We shall try now to determine just where the
problem lies, and we shall consider a solution
that our theory of graphic representation does not
encompass but that it does lead to.

Two-dimensional models in linguistics

Before we can do so, we must reduce our taxonomy of graphic representation in linguistics still
further. For when we consider the fact--which we
have noted a number of times--that all figures in
linguistics are built out of only two art elements,
line and space, the number of basic types shrinks
from three to two. These two are branching diagrams and tables.

How does this come about? Partly as a result
of the scant vocabulary of linguistic representation; partly as a result of the existence of two
major themes in linguistic analysis, constituent
analysis (of which genesis and taxonomy are
special kinds) and componential analysis (of which
conflation is a special kind); they correspond
respectively to branching diagrams and tables.
The branching diagram *par excellence* is, of course,
the tree; the dynamic, hierarchical quality inherent in tree diagrams is the heart of constituent
analysis. The table *par excellence* is the matrix;
the static, nonhierarchical quality inherent in
matrix diagrams is the heart of componential
analysis. The two themes are thus reflected in
two kinds of figures, two styles of linguistic
architecture.[20]
     The third type of figure, box diagrams, can
easily be construed as either branching diagrams
or tables. This is clearly the case with block
diagrams, which are isomorphic with either a tree
(for the meaning of constituent analysis) or a
matrix (for the meaning of conflation). They are
clearly built on an armature of one or the other:

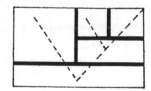   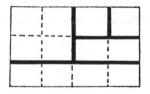

constituent analysis   conflation

Thus block diagrams are at most allomorphs--
better, allographs--of the tree or the matrix--
that is, of branching diagrams or tables. So is

the Chinese box, isomorphic with a tree for
constituent analysis:

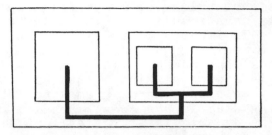

More accurately, it is isomorphic with two trees,
or rather with a sort of Rorschach tree, the top
and bottom halves of which, however, do not differ:

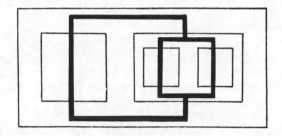

        Isomorphism is important because mere synonymy
is not sufficient to reduce two figures to allo-
morphs of a single figure. If it were, the correspondences between figures and meanings for graphic
representation in linguistics would be easily un-
raveled. Isomorphic representations are as close
to the same figure as it is possible to be without
being the same figure. Neither adds anything to
what is represented by the other; neither subtracts
anything from what is represented by the other; the
figures express the same meaning in the same way.
(For conflation block diagrams, this is not quite
true; but they are clearly tables just as matrices
are, for they are only matrices in which empty
cells are given a particular interpretation. It
is this interpretation that changes the meaning
from componential analysis to conflation.)

The cube is more difficult. Because it is
constructed out of line and space, and because of
the way in which its parts express the meaning of
componential analysis, it can be read as a branching diagram,

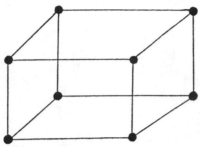

in which points are the units of the system and
the lines branching from point to point carry
shared features. This is the visual ambiguity of
the cube. But there is also a sense in which the
cube, read as a three-dimensional figure, is a
tabular representation, inasmuch as it is the
representation on a fixed figure of systems which
vary. The number of features is fixed at three,
and the number of units at eight, because the
number of dimensions in the figure is three, and
the number of corners, eight. The position of
the units is also fixed, and so empty space has
meaning.
    The possibility of saying something about
system or pattern by letting a slot stand empty
is characteristic of tables as against branching
diagrams. In a tree (with the exception of a tree
for componential analysis, a key) there is no way
to express the lack of a unit which ought to be
there, to express conspicuous absence. Given a
tree and a unit which is lacking in the system
represented by that tree, who can say, without
knowing in advance the structure of the system
represented, just where it is missing? More important, who can infer from the shape of the tree
that there *is* something missing? In a cube, on
the other hand, the absence of a unit is

immediately felt, as we saw in the figure from
Austerlitz. Moreover, the cube is isomorphic with
other fixed figures more table-like in appearance.
Thus

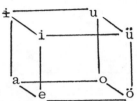

may equally well be represented as

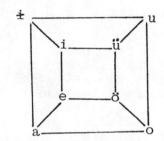

or turned inside-out (Conklin, personal communication) to

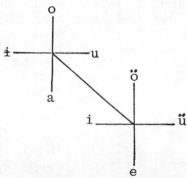

Whether the cube is a branching diagram or a
table, then, depends on how it is read. The
point is that it, like the other box diagrams,
can be fitted into a two-part scheme consisting

of branching diagrams and tables; it is essentially a two-dimensional construction.   In
fact, the very ambiguity of the cube suggests
that this two-part scheme is not a dichotomy
but a continuum, the two poles of which are
two essentially opposite figures.
     By now it is apparent that for this two-
part scheme to work, whether it is a dichotomy
or a continuum, the concept of branching diagrams must be enlarged to include more than
trees, as the concept of tables has been
enlarged to include different kinds of fixed
figures.   In enlarging the notion of branching
diagrams to embrace all the kinds found in
linguistics, we shall need to depart from the
definition of tree diagrams established so far.
     We must first of all dispense with the
requirement of a unique beginner.   There will
then be room for such branching diagrams as
the vines of Morin and O'Malley:

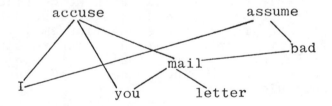

There is after all no *a priori* reason why
constituent-analysis trees should have a unique
beginner: a great many sentences in fact
"begin" at more than one spot.   The sentence
above, for instance, is no more than

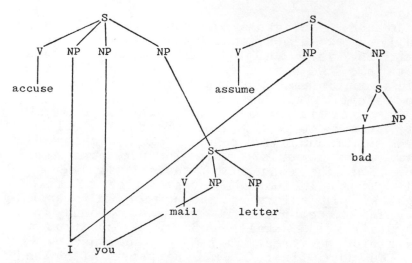

(Morin, personal communication)

The requirement of a unique beginner is a requirement of meaning--the meaning of taxonomy--and not
of form. This becomes clear when we consider the
reading imposed on tree diagrams by dependency
grammar. The graphic representation employed by
Tesnière, for example, bears a strong resemblance
to the vines of Morin and O'Malley, though the
latter were developed independently (Morin, personal communication):

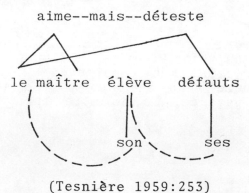

(Tesnière 1959:253)

That the resemblance is no more than that, how-
ever--a *graphic* similarity only--is apparent from
discussions of the meaning of such trees in dependency grammar generally.[21] Morin and O'Malley's
diagram expresses the complicated network of relations holding among various constituents in the
deep structure--relations of various kinds--and
expresses them in such a way as to avoid repeating
elements (such as *I* or *you* in the sentence given
above) simply because they participate in more
than one relation.

     The diagrams of dependency grammar, on the
other hand, express one sort of relation only:
that of dependency, or government. As a consequence, the tree in dependency grammar differs
radically not only from that of Morin and O'Malley
but also from that of transformational grammar,
and in fact from constituent-analysis trees in
general. Essentially, dependency grammar supple-
ments phrase-structure grammar by making room for
the expression of government: Robinson (1970b:268)
quotes Postal, who points out that, in a PS rule
like NP ⟶ T N, the information that N is the
head is necessarily lost.[22] Yet this ultimately
imposes on the tree diagram a reading altogether
different from that of constituent analysis. Here
the vertical dimension means "dependency" rather
than "constituency," so that the branches are to
be construed, reading down, as "x governs y," and,
reading up, as "y is dependent on x." This is in
contrast to the readings required for constituent-
analysis trees, which are respectively "x dominates (in the sense of "contains") y" and "y is a
constituent (a subset) of x." The horizontal dimension then has no meaning in dependency trees,
since no longer, as in constituent-analysis diagrams, are elements on the same horizantal subsets
of the same (immediately dominating) set.

     Thus dependency grammar imposes a different
reading of the graphic elements of the tree. The
difference is underscored by the graphic variant
used by such linguists as Anderson (1971a, 1971b),

Hays (1964), and Robinson (1970a, 1970b), in which
slanting, solid-line branches represent relations
of dependency, while straight, broken-line branches
represent lexical realization. A diagram such as

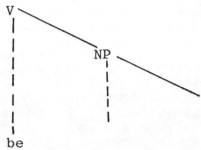

is to be read: "V, realized as *be*, governs NP."
(The distinction between broken lines for realization and solid lines for constituency is to be
found in constituent-analysis trees as well; but
since it is not possible for a node to participate
simultaneously in constituency and realization, the
graphic distinction is redundant. What is instead
relied on to give the information that lexical
realization, rather than constituency, is intended,
is the convention that terminal elements stand in
that relation to the non-branching nodes by which
they are immediately dominated.[23]) Clearly, then,
the reading imposed by dependency grammar constitutes a fifth meaning for the tree. Does it therefore depart from all other meanings for the figure?
It would seem so: government is a concept apart
from the concepts of genesis, taxonomy, componential analysis, and constituent analysis--all of
which share, as we have seen, a least common denom-
inator, the notion of successive replacement,
linked at least to some degree in each with the
notion of sets and subsets. Dependency trees, in
contrast, express a notion that does not at all
include the idea of successive replacement; to the
contrary, it precludes it: for an element to govern
or be governed by another, both must be present.

And this idea is, moreover, expressed simultaneously with another--that of realization--which is not
(as in constituent-analysis trees) automatically
entailed by the first, but wholly independent of
it.

   It has become apparent, from the examples
given above, that in dispensing with the requirement that a tree have a unique beginner, we must
dispense as well with the requirement that its
branches not converge. This, too, seems to be a
restriction imposed by the meaning of taxonomy; and
this, too, is better foregone for syntactic analysis.
Both the vines of Morin and O'Malley and the tree
diagrams of dependency grammar are likely to give
rise to a network--a tree without a unique beginner and with converging branches. In Morin and
O'Malley's diagram, for instance, convergence at
the lower S-node is expressive of the double constituent function of that S, as object of both
accuse and *assume*, while the redivergence of the
branches expresses the fact that the lower S itself
decomposes into constituents. In Tesnière's diagram, convergence expresses the double dependency
of *le maître* (on both *aime* and *déteste*); and it is
not hard to imagine, for the kind of diagram employed by other versions of dependency grammar,
cases in which convergence would be necessary--
that is, wherever, in more complicated structures,
an element governs or is governed by more than one
other element.[24]

   Admitting convergence makes the definition of
branching diagrams roomy enough to accommodate as
well some other, less obviously tree-like figures.
These include Chomsky's finite-state diagram,

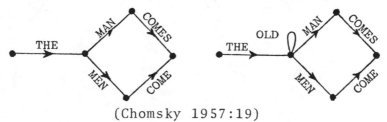

(Chomsky 1957:19)

--really a left-to-right tree, a tree lying on
its side, with convergence. They also include
"morpheme order diagrams" (Hoenigswald 1950)
such as the "freightyard,"

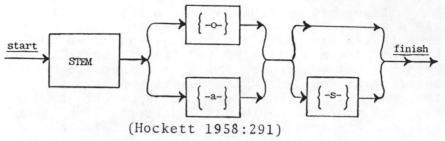

(Hockett 1958:291)

and the "maze":

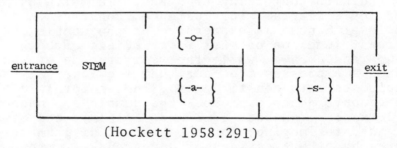

(Hockett 1958:291)

These are alternatives to a figure like the
"rollercoaster,"

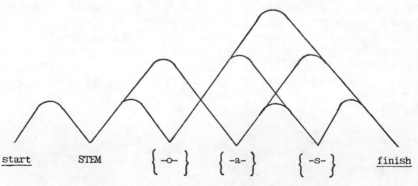

(Hockett 1958:291)

which, because it sets out all the morphemic
alternatives in a row, must use varying configurations of line to express possible combinations
of morphemes. As Hockett (1958:292) points out,
the rollercoaster cannot, like the freightyard and
the maze, display morphemes paradigmatically along
the vertical dimension at the same time as it
represents them syntagmatically as possible combinations of morphemes. The freightyard and the
maze are isomorphic--in fact, very nearly identical--
figures, differing in that the freightyard is
explicitly treelike in form. (The freightyard is
actually a directed graph, as we shall see later
on). Both the freightyard and the maze, however,
could with little alteration become a left-to-right
converging tree:

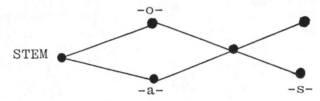

     Weinreich (1966:408) points out that conver-
gence diagrams are the alternative to rearranging
the order of elements on the tree. A fixed order
of elements, he says, is incompatible with a fixed
configuration of branching. We must amend this to
add: unless elements are repeated. Katz and
Postal's lexical entry tree for *bachelor*, for
example, hangs onto both a fixed order of semantic
features and a fixed configuration of branching (a
tree that fulfills the two requirements we have just
jettisoned, those of a unique beginner and non-con-
vergence)--but only at the expense of repeating
features. If we allow convergence, on the other
hand, we need not repeat features to preserve their
order:

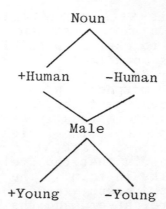

Similarly, the problem of designing a branching diagram that simultaneously represents the
hierarchy of features and allows to be inferred
all and only the correct implicational relations
among them, is very simply solved by permitting
convergence. A convergence diagram obviates the
difficulties posed, for instance, by the representation of the lexical feature hierarchy from
Bever and Rosenbaum discussed in Chapter 1:

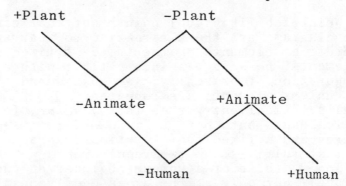

Such a representation not only captures the essential unique implication which concerns Bever and
Rosenbaum--that is, [+Human] implies [+Animate]
implies [-Plant]--but also conveys accurately the
non-unique implications of [-Human] (which implies
either [+Animate] or [-Animate]) and [-Animate]

(which implies either [+Plant] or [-Plant]). Moreover, such a representation is isomorphic with the
facts of the case: for a blending of two meanings,
taxonomy and componential analysis, a blending of
two trees--one reading down, the abstract taxonomic
relation among the features-as-classes; another
reading up, the practical implicational relation
among the features-as-components. (In its double-
ness, the convergence diagram recalls the "Rorschach" tree used by Pike; the former is a better
representation for the theoretical concept we are
discussing here insofar as it expresses graphically the notion of a blending of two different analytic techniques, while the latter expresses
graphically the notion of two different applications of the *same* analytic technique, that of
taxonomy.) Clearly, then, the difficulties of
lexical representation discussed by Bever and
Rosenbaum arise at least in part from insisting
on an unsuitable representation, from denying the
admissibility of convergence in tree diagrams. A
convergence diagram is a better expression of the
theoretical concept--in actuality, as we have seen,
a double concept--involved; and, as Chomsky and
Halle point out, "the more direct the relationship
between classificatory and . . . -etic matrices,
the less complex--the more highly valued--will be
the resulting grammar" (1968:381). Thus we have,
again, a demonstration of the influence of model
upon theory.
     The third and last alteration needed to make
the definition of tree diagrams fit all kinds of
branching diagrams concerns directionality. Let
such diagrams be either dynamic or static, either
with or without directionality, and the definition
is capacious enough to include network diagrams.
(This is the sort of figure which the cube turns
into if it is read as a configuration of point and
line.) Networks generally express componential
analysis, as in the following example:

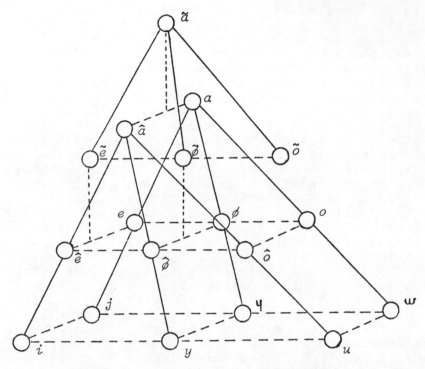

(Jakobson and Lotz 1949:157)

If parallel lines are used, as they are here, to
express the same feature, the figure can convey an
analysis in several features. Where most of the
branching diagrams we have looked at are dynamic,
having a beginning (or several beginnings) and an
end, network diagrams are static. They have
neither beginning nor end.

The definition of branching diagrams that has
emerged so far is no more than a definition of
graphs.[25] For what is a graph but the joining of
points by lines? What we have called dynamic branching diagrams--trees, branching diagrams with more
than one beginner, and convergence diagrams--are
"directed graphs," graphs with a definite irreversible direction for every "edge" (Ore 1963:53).[26]

The directedness of directed graphs is usually
shown by arrows, as in

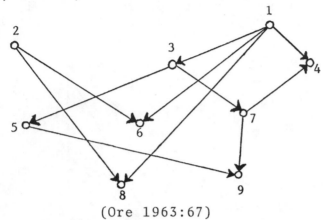

(Ore 1963:67)

Morin and O'Malley's vine diagram (which, as its
designers point out [182], is a type of directed
graph) would be

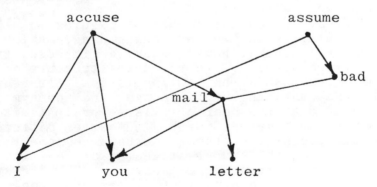

Hockett's various morpheme structure diagrams
would be

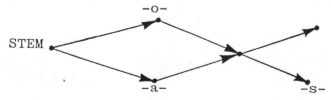

What we have called network diagrams, in contrast, are undirected graphs (Ore 1963:52). They
would look just as they do ordinarily, like the
network for Jakobson's componential analysis of
Russian declension,

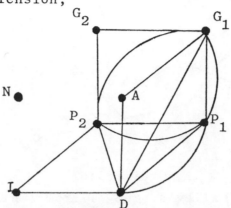

(The chart of correspondences between form and
meaning for graphic representation in linguistics
is a network diagram.)
     We have pared the number of figures in use
for linguistics to two, branching diagrams (or
graphs) and tables, having gone, as it were, from
the surface structure to the deep structure of
graphic representation in linguistics. It seems
clear that the tangle of synonymy and homonymy
can be laid at the door of this severely limited
inventory of figures. With a number of different
analytic techniques (though perhaps no more than
variations on the two great themes of constituent
analysis and componential analysis, they are still
different), with a number of different schools and
theories and periods of linguistic science, how
can such slender resources stretch far enough?
Moreover, it is likely that the influence of
graphic representation on the development of linguistic theory depends on the figures available.
What allows the reduction of all the figures in
linguistics to two is the restriction of the vocabulary of graphic representation to the two art

elements of line and space, coupled with the limitations of two-dimensionality. In a sense, then,
the problem of graphic representation suggests its
own solution: widen the resources of representation; increase the dimensions to three.

Three-dimensional models in linguistics

     "The heart of all major discoveries in the
physical sciences," says Toulmin (1953:34), "is
the discovery of novel methods of representation,
and so of fresh techniques by which inferences can
be drawn." Three-dimensional models are certainly
novel methods of representation for linguistic science; but, as we have suggested, they are in a sense
the natural inheritors of graphic representation:
they grow out of the kind of representation they
replace; for three-dimensional representation
simply expands the vocabulary of art elements to
include volume. And three-dimensional models furnish fresh techniques by which inferences can be
drawn about a linguistic *explicandum*--a fresh
neutral analogy. Not only do three-dimensional
models open up new territory to be explored, but
they also suggest points at which it would be wise
to re-examine old ground. They can correct the
neutral analogy furnished by two-dimensional models
in which territory was wrongly claimed for the
positive analogy, resulting in the unwarranted
development of linguistic theory. Three-dimensional
alternatives to graphic representation are thus
indirect evidence for the claim that graphic representation influences the direction taken by
linguistic theory.
     We have already had evidence of the necessity
for--indeed, the inevitability of--three-dimensional
models in linguistics, in the attempt to get over
into three dimensions that is seen in the modification of transformational-generative theory. The
notions of rule, of the transformational cycle, of
the dichotomy between deep and surface structure,

all represent such an attempt. The dichotomy
between deep and surface structure in particular--
imposing the requirement of holding simultaneously
in the mind two mutually exclusive views of the
explicandum--is not restricted to transformational
grammar. Stratificational grammar is another
theory that implicitly imposes such a requirement:
as its very name suggests, it takes at any given
moment in the analysis a multiple view of the
datum. Still another is dependency grammar. This
is apparent in the work of Tesnière; such a
representation as

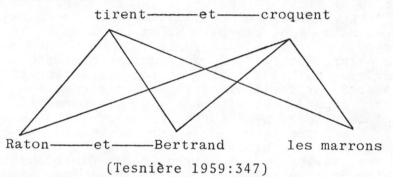

(Tesnière 1959:347)

is intended as collapsing or telescoping deep and
surface structure. As Tesnière points out, this
diagram "fait intervenir quatre phrases, qu'il est
parfaitement possible d'additionner":

Raton		tire		les marrons
Raton			croque	les marrons
	Bertrand	tire		les marrons
	Bertrand		croque	les marrons

Raton et Bertrand tirent et croquent les marrons

Tesnière himself insists on the fundamental dis-
crepancy between the two-dimensional model and the
multi-dimensional *explicandum*: "Il y a donc anti-
nomie entre l'ordre structural, qui est à *plusieurs*
dimensions (réduites à deux dans le stemma), et

l'ordre linéaire, qui est à une dimension" (21
[italics mine]).
     Transformational-generative theory has so
come to rely on the notion of movement, expressed
as rules, as to make of it a productive device in
every instance where the two-dimensional model
falls short of the *explicandum*--that is, where
exploration of the neutral analogy it presents
suggests modification of the theory. An example
is the modification of the concept of markedness
proposed by Chomsky and Halle (1968) and imple-
mented in a modified form for syntax by Lakoff
(1970). Chomsky and Halle's revised markedness
theory replaces the old +/-/0 values in phonological matrices (grid diagrams) for lexical items
with the values *m*[arked]/*u*[nmarked]/+/- and the
addition of marking conventions. The marking conventions, not part of the grammar but rather "universal rules of interpretation" (403), serve to
convert *m* and *u* values to + and - ; they are thus
rules upon rules. These marking conventions, moreover, are extremely complex: they are context
sensitive (e.g., "in initial position before a
consonant, the consonant that is [*u* continuant] is
interpreted as [+ continuant]; in other positions
it is interpreted as [- continuant]" [412]); they
incorporate the whole set of implicational relations existing among features (410); and they serve
as the measure of the "naturalness" of phonological
systems (411) and phonological rules (420). Such
complexity argues strongly for the view that these
rules add a dimension to the grammar.
     The notional addition of a dimension, though
it gives evidence of the necessity of three-dimensional models for linguistic theory, is nonetheless
merely notional; it remains to demonstrate the usefulness of actual three-dimensional models in linguistics. The first of two three-dimensional
models that we shall consider here is a phrase-
structure mobile. The design is William G. Moulton's
(personal communication); it consists in putting a
phrase-structure (immediate-constituent) tree into

three dimensions, suspended by its unique beginner,
S, so that it floats in space:

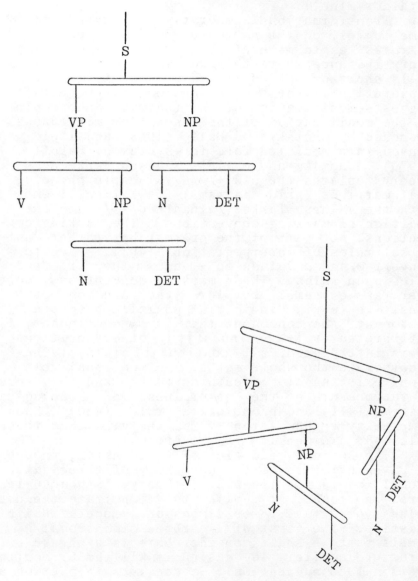

We can learn from it not only about the
explicandum, English sentences, but also about
the influence of tree diagrams on linguistic
theory. The problems presented by tree diagrams
include the ordering of constituents in the deep
structure; the difficulty of representing discontinuous constituents; the necessity for positing
such transformations as pruning, extraposition,
subject-raising. All are rooted in the linearity
of two-dimensional representation. It is reasonable, then, to suppose that transplanting the tree
diagram from a two-dimensional medium into a three-
dimensional one will remove these difficulties.
      The order of constituents in deep structure
is one drawback that the phrase-structure mobile
does not have. Because the tree is suspended by
its beginner, the terminal elements--the deep
structure constituents--hang free; they shift this
way and that as the mobile moves, so that it is
impossible to fix them in any order. It is important that this happens without change in the
hierarchical structure imposed on the *explicandum*
by its analysis into immediate constituents:
because this hierarchical structure lies wholly
on the vertical dimension, it is preserved. The
model of the phrase-structure mobile, then, allows
us to conceive of, to visualize, constituent analysis without ordered constituents. It expunges
from the neutral analogy the potentially misleading
element of linear order.
      Representation of discontinuous constituents
is another difficulty that the phrase structure
mobile avoids. Because there is no linear order
of terminal elements, there is no need to grapple
with the problem of discontinuous constituents,
terminal elements that violate that order. The
ultimate constituents--the terminal elements--are
not linked by the exigencies of two-dimensionality
into a continuous chain. Even constituents in the
same construction are related not horizontally but
vertically, by virtue of the hierarchical structure

imposed by constituent analysis; in the phrase-
structure mobile we have been looking at, for
instance, the two constituents

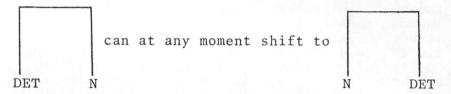

and back again; this in no way alters their relationship to each other or to the other elements in
the sentence. Conversely, if we have a sentence
like *I looked him up*, in which *looked . . . up* is
a discontinuous construction, we must, in two-
dimensional representation, disentangle the two
constructions that make up the sentence:

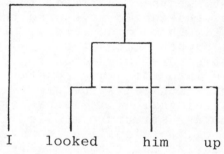

In three-dimensional representation, the constituents would not be constrained by linear order.
They would float free, bound only by the ties of
hierarchical structure along the vertical dimension.
Since constituents are not continuous to begin with,
there is no need to discontinue constituents that
have been fortuitously thrown together.
    This is, admittedly, a less clear case of the
advantages to be gained by increasing two dimensions to three. In the first place, one pays a
price for the advantage of not having to represent
discontinuity, and that is not being able to represent continuity. It is not possible to show the

linearity that is, after all, characteristic of
speech if not of grammatical structure. Thus there
is, in the second place, the question of whether
the neutral analogy furnished by the phrase-structure mobile is not in its own way misleading. For
if the counterpoint between linear order and hierarchical structure is characteristic of language,
it is misleading for the three-dimensional model
to indicate only hierarchical structure. The
phrase-structure mobile suggests that the aspect
of the neutral analogy furnished by the two-dimensional model that concerns the continuity of terminal elements ought to be consigned to the negative
analogy. The question is, what is it we are investigating? What is the *explicandum* for which the
phrase-structure mobile is an analogue? If it is
grammatical structure--deep structure--and not
speech--surface structure--then the mobile is a
better model than the two-dimensional tree.

The problem of such transformations as pruning, extraposition, raising, and the like, is only
partly circumvented by the phrase-structure mobile.
We should still like to delete nodes that do not
branch, that is, horizontal bars with nothing hang-
ing from them; to remove segments and hang them
elsewhere; to call moving a segment higher up on
the structure "raising" it. If these are misleading notions, if they reflect nothing in the
explicandum, no processes that actually go on in
the world (wherever it is) of grammar, then they
are the point at which the three-dimensional model
fails us, the point at which it is outgrown. The
important thing is that the two-dimensional figure
does function as a model for linguistic science,
and that there does lie a better model just beyond
it. That going from a two-dimensional to a three-
dimensional model, a mere change of representation,
removes apparent theoretical givens like the order
of constituents in deep structure, shows the very
real influence of graphic representation on
linguistic theory.

The second of our three-dimensional models for
linguistics is a torus for phonological space. A

torus, a geometrical solid whose surface is formed
by rotating a circle about a vertical axis (Hilbert
and Cohn-Vossen 1952:200), looks like this:

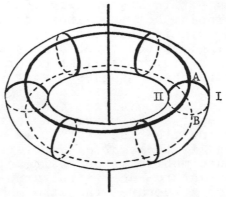

(Hilbert and Cohn-Vossen 1952:200)

In a torus model of phonological space, the usual
matrix arrangement for consonants,

f	θ	ç	x	xf
p	t	k̂	k	kp
b	d	ĝ	g	gb
v	ð	γ̂	γ	γv

is first wrapped around from top to bottom to form
a cylinder:

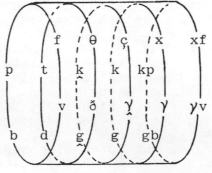

It is then wrapped from left to right as well, so
that the front consonants abut the back ones:

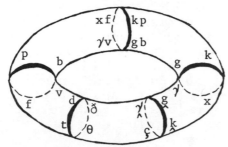

       The three-dimensional torus is a more
accurate model for phonological space than the
two-dimensional matrix for two reasons: first,
the three-dimensional model allows a fuller and
more accurate expression of the componential analysis of sound systems, whether it is traditional
articulatory analysis or distinctive feature analysis; second, the three-dimensional model reflects
better the facts of sound change. Before we dis-
cuss the reasons why the three-dimensional model
is a better fit for the *explicandum* of phonological space, however, we shall look more closely at
its construction.
       The circle is the one simple geometric shape
that did not figure in our taxonomy of diagrams in
linguistics; it *does* figure among the forerunners
of the torus, in Grimm's *Kreislauf*.

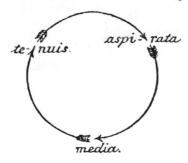

(Schleicher 1888:97)

The circular configuration reflects the facts of
sound change: the Germanic and High German Consonant Shifts, in which Indo-European *Aspiratae* (A)
[bʰ dʰ gʰ] became Germanic *Mediae* (M) [b d g] and
subsequently Old High German *Tenues* (T) [p t k];
Indo-European *Mediae* [b d g] became Germanic *Tenues*
[p t k] and subsequently Old High German *Aspirata*
(pᶠ tˢ x];   and Indo-European *Tenues* [p t k] became
Germanic *Aspiratae* [f θ x] and subsequently Old
High German *Mediae* [b d g].   Representing these
sound changes by a circle,

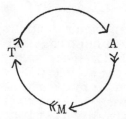

collapses into a single configuration the following:

$$A \gg\longrightarrow M \gg\longrightarrow T$$

$$M \gg\longrightarrow T \gg\longrightarrow A$$

$$T \gg\longrightarrow A \gg\longrightarrow M$$

The *Kreislauf* constitutes a longitudinal section
of the torus.   Slicing through the torus from top
to bottom yields

The *Kreislauf*, then, must also be equivalent to a
matrix arrangement, wrapped from top to bottom,
that is,

p	t	k
b	d	g
bh	dh	gh

can become

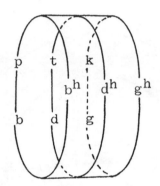

The other direction, wrapping from left to right, was proposed by Moulton (MS) as an alternative to the matrix, to account for sound changes like the shift from Old English /x/ to Modern English /f/ (as in *tōh* > *tough*) and to accommodate sounds with double articulation (for instance, [kp], [gb]). In both cases, only the two ends of the spectrum along the horizontal in the matrix are involved; the problem, then, is how to get from one end of the matrix to the other without traversing the middle. Moulton's solution is to curve phonological space--though still in two dimensions--so that every row in the matrix becomes a circle:

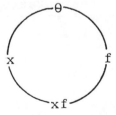

(Moulton MS:20)

The whole horizontal dimension of the matrix would
of course be involved; this does not necessarily
yield a three-dimensional model, however. The
result could be a set of concentric circles:

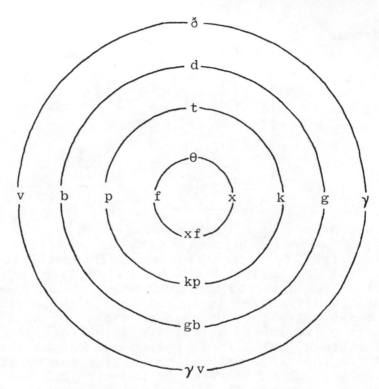

This is presumably what Moulton has in mind, since
he at no time mentions a three-dimensional model.
But for our purposes, the three-dimensional wrapping of the matrix from left to right as well is
the better conception.
     Among the reasons for preferring the three-
dimensional model for phonological space is that
it is a better representation of the componential
analysis of sound systems. The ordering of sounds
sharing the same place of articulation on the torus
was suggested by the *Kreislauf*. The usual order of
sounds in the matrix is:

p

b

f

v

or, in terms of articulatory features,

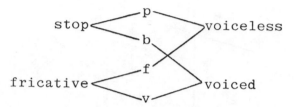

The ordering in the torus, in contrast, allows any
sounds sharing a feature to be contiguous:

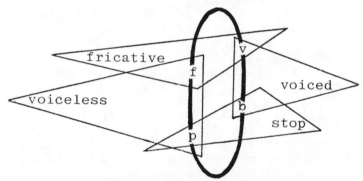

In terms of distinctive feature theory, each cir-
cle--each cross-section of the torus--constitutes
a correlation:

Wrapping the matrix from top to bottom, then, allows a better expression of componential analysis;
so does wrapping it from left to right. It not

only provides a natural place to put sounds like
[kp] in a traditional articulatory analysis, as
Moulton's curved phonological space was designed
in part to do. It also makes contiguous the
sounds that share the feature [+Grave], which
the matrix cannot do.

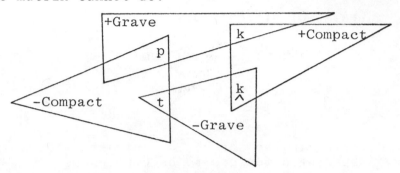

     The second reason for preferring the torus to
the matrix is that it mirrors the historical facts
of sound change. It is already clear that this is
so for the two sound shifts diagrammed by the
Kreislauf. It is true as well for a number of
sound changes involving--heretofore inexplicably--
the two ends of the matrix without going through
the middle, like the shift from Old English /x/ to
Modern English /f/, inexplicable in terms of the
two-dimensional matrix model. What route did the
change take through phonological space? Did /x/
creep around *behind* the figure? And what was it
doing travelling in the wrong direction (from
right to left) in the first place? Theories of
sound change developed from the matrix model can,
it is true, explain such changes by positing intermediate stages in the shift--for instance, [x] >
[θ] > [f]; but there is not always evidence for
such intermediate stages--indeed, in many cases,
the evidence tells against them (Moulton MS:20).
Moreover, they cannot account for the fact that
the sounds travel in the wrong direction. It is
this sort of sound change that the wrapping of the
matrix from left to right is designed to accommodate.

Both of the three-dimensional models we have
looked at, the phrase-structure mobile and the torus for phonological space, are improvements on
two-dimensional models, the tree and the matrix
respectively--the two kinds of figures current in
linguistics. Both grow out of two-dimensional
representation. Neither is without its flaws:
the phrase-structure mobile, while it escapes some
of the pitfalls of tree diagrams, does not escape
others; the torus, though it is a better fit for
the *explicandum* of phonological space, is an over-
simplified representation of it insofar as it does
not have room for vowels and semi-vowels.

Thus our theory of graphic representation,
with its double perspective of the philosophy of
science and the principles of design, has led us
back again to the question with which we began.
What is it in graphic representation that enables
it to furnish models for linguistic science?
Though our theory does not solve all the problems
it uncovers in graphic representation in linguistics, it does uncover them; though it does not
answer all the questions it raises, it does raise
them. It is clear that as long as graphic representation furnishes linguistic science with models,
as long as it influences the development of linguistic theory, the solution to the problems of
model-building lies in more model-building. It
lies in the direction in which our theory of
graphic representation leads: in the understanding
of the function of models according to the philosophy of science; in the understanding of the construction of models according to the principles of
design.

Notes

¹ Maher (1966:9, note 3) names several works perpetuating the myth of a Darwinian linguistics; his inclusion of Greenberg 1957 is questionable.

² In a letter from Darwin to Lyell, dated September 23, 1860 (Francis Darwin 1888:341–344), there appears an upside-down version:

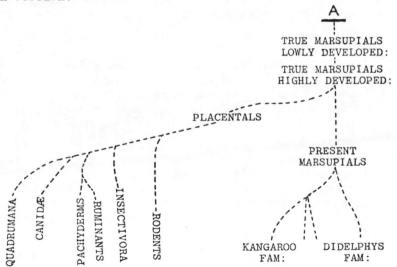

³ Chomsky and Halle (1968:295) are aware that such feature classes are "intersecting categories," though the redundancy rules inferred from the usual nonconverging feature

hierarchy in works such as Chomsky 1965 do not appear to
reflect this awareness.

[4] This blending of two different theoretical statements
about the same data is hinted at in Chomsky and Halle's distinction, for phonetic features, between a "classificatory
function" and a "phonetic function" (1968:298). In the
former, features are class-names and therefore abstract, and
it is only in this use that their values are restricted to
binary; in the latter, features correspond to aspects of
phonetic reality and admit of n-ary gradations in value.
Clearly, the fusion of these two uses is involved in the
problem of lexical-feature hierarchy discussed above: it
seems likely that the hierarchy imposed on feature-classes
by reading down the tree belongs to the first, or abstract,
use, while the redundancy rules or implicational relations
to be got from the tree by reading up belong to the second,
or practical use.

[5] Allen (1953:8) draws a distinction between a syllabic
"method of writing" and the essentially phonemic analysis
"underlying it and actually set out . . . in the *varṇa-samāmnāya*.

[6] Jespersen's an(t)alphabetic notation (1889) will not
be considered here. The matrix does not appear in it, perhaps because the characters are concatenations rather than
unit symbols, making a tabular arrangement unwieldy.

[7] Conflation arrangements (as opposed to actual diagrams)
of inflectional paradigms are often found in pedagogical gram-
mars and are of long standing; see for instance Whitney's
Sanskrit grammar, first published in 1879 (Whitney 1889).
Such arrangements are arrived at by shifting the case endings
for each paradigm until the result is blocks of like endings
as in Jakobson's diagrams.

[8] Classification even along a continuum is difficult.
For a notion of the model as central, see Black 1962, Campbell 1921, Hesse 1966, Toulmin 1953; for a notion of the

model as peripheral, see Braithwaite 1953, Hesse's (1966) discussion of Duhem, and perhaps Nagel 1961. Lachman's (1963: 79-83) classification of the uses of models is evidence that all of these views are useful at one time or another.

[9] With regard to whether the analogizing consists in illuminating the unfamiliar by comparing it with the familiar, or *vice versa*--a debate not to be pursued here--see Campbell (1921:84), Nagel (1961:107), Rosenblueth and Wiener (1945:317) *versus* Black (1962:233), Toulmin (1953:20). "Familiar" and "unfamiliar" are, after all, relative: the relation of material analogy remains the same whichever view is taken. Of the various *types* of models little need be said beyond the fact that this work deals with neither "physical" (or scale) models nor "formal" (or mathematical) ones. It is difficult to choose a name for the type of model it does deal with, variously termed "symbolic," "material," and "analogue." The subject of types of models is pursued in Beckner (1959: 33-36, 52-53), Black (1962:222-229), Chapanes (1963:109-110), Kaplan (1964:266-268), and Rosenblueth and Wiener (1945:317).

[10] The difference is one of emphasis, reflecting the degree of concern about possible abuse of the model, either by choosing a poor one or by letting it usurp the place of the theory (Braithwaite 1953:93-96). Black (1962:236), Campbell (Hesse 1966:3-4, 98-99), Kaplan (1964:274-275), Kuhn (1962:184), Nagel (1961:112), and Toulmin (1953:37-39) agree on these two functions, though their terminology differs.

[11] Extension and development correspond to the two directions suggested in the philosophy of science for the influence of the model on scientific theory; see Black (1962: 228-229, 241), Hesse (1966:98-99), Kaplan (1964:274-275), Kuhn (1962:24), Nagel (1961:112-114), Toulmin (1953:39).

[12] The reference in transformational theory of the term "extraposition" to the tree diagram itself is clear by contrast with Jespersen's use of the term. While Jespersen defines "extraposition" with reference to sentences--"a word, or a group of words, is placed, as it were, outside the sen-

tence as if it had nothing to do there," as in *As to an Abyssinian victory, that is out of the question* (1937:35)--transformationalists define it with reference to the figure, as the placing of a group of constituents, usually an embedded sentence, on the outside (the extreme right-hand side) of the diagram.

[13] All of these transformation-types are to be found in Stockwell, Schachter, and Partee (1973), as well as elsewhere in the literature.

[14] Compare Lyons (1968:155-156) for a discussion of the meaning of "generative" as (1) "predictive;" and (2) "explicit."

[15] Pruning has become a widely-accepted theoretical modification, not only for transformational-generative theory *per se* but also for other grammatical theories, such as dependency grammar: Robinson (1970b:282), for instance, proposes a revised S-pruning convention.

[16] Transformational-generative grammar is not, of course, the only theory current in linguistics to draw its terms from the model or from a metaphor attached to the model. Stratificational grammar, for example (the very name of which reflects a geological metaphor), employs terms like "knot pattern" that reflect what goes on graphically, in the diagrams (Lamb 1966). Other grammatical theories that make use of transformations tend also to name them from the figure--for example, the "infrajection" transformations of case grammar (Fillmore 1968:23, n. 29), the "raising" transformations of dependency grammar (Anderson 1971b).

[17] The art elements go by different names, and not all treatments include them all. Kepes (1944:23) lists point, shape, line, position, color, value, texture; Anderson (1961), only line, shape, texture, color, and motion. Klee (1961:76) gives the "formal elements of graphic art" as simply "points, and linear, plane, and spatial energies."

[18] The works of Anderson (1961), Kepes (1944), Klee (1961), and Scott (1951) are general treatments. More specific treatments, handbooks of graphic design and graphic designers' manuals, are concerned with typography or with the application of design principles to advertising. It seemed best, therefore, to consult general works and construct from them a "handbook" for graphic representation in linguistics.

[19] The principle of iconic relations is one of Chao's "ten requirements for good symbols"(1968:210-227); the others, applying chiefly to unit symbols such as orthographic characters, are not useful for our purposes.

[20] We shall leave Reed-Kellogg diagrams out of the discussion that follows. They defy classification, because they are, in both form and meaning, so very complicated. Their form is an elaborate code in the shape and slant of lines; their meaning comprises not only constituent analysis but also constituent function, and encompasses simultaneously deep and surface structure.

[21] Though Robinson (1970b:260) asserts that Tesnière's is a dependency grammar, it differs somewhat from other versions of dependency grammar such as those of Anderson (1971b), Fillmore (1968), and Robinson. As these latter are more explicit regarding the reading of tree diagrams, the discussion that follows draws largely on them.

[22] Dependency grammar has various theoretical affinities: with transformational-generative grammar (both employ phrase-structure rules and transformations); with tagmemics (Fillmore [1968:88] notes the ease of conversion between a dependency grammar and the slot-filler notion of tagmemic theory); with Reed-Kellogg school grammar (both are concerned to express notions of grammatical function--modification and government--and Reed-Kellogg diagrams are graphically the literal expression of slot and filler). It is important to note, however, that these are affinities of theory--of notions and concepts--rather than affinities of representation. Reed-

Kellogg diagrams and tagmemic notation especially have
little in common graphically with dependency trees.

[23] In Fillmore's original formulation (Fillmore 1968)
of case grammar, it was by no means clear that the vertical
dimension of his tree was to be construed as dependency;
Robinson (1970a:64) substantiates Fillmore's suspicion that
his base rules "mix categorical notions with relational
(functional) ones in a way that Chomsky sought to avoid by
defining functions in terms of configurations of categories,
rather than by directly labelling them." Fillmore himself
finally suggested a dependency reading for trees in case
grammar and an alternative design for the tree so read.
Since the case categories may well be, in actual function,
simply "*labels on the branches that link P with the various
NP's* [italics his]," then "one may just as well represent
these relationships more directly by replacing the node P
by the V" (87)--as in the diagrams of dependency grammar in
general.

[24] This need not necessarily mean lengthier constructions; for more complex notions of modification, more complex
diagrams--for example,

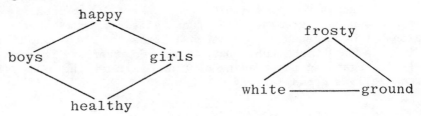

(Goodman 1961:54)

[25] It should be noted that the mathematics here is of
the most rudimentary sort: it is touched on at all only in
order to illuminate the graphic nature of what we have been
calling tree diagrams. There are treatments of graph theory
and applications of these and other mathematical concepts to
some of the representation used in linguistics (see, for
instance, Zierer 1970). This book is not intended to replace them, but rather to approach the subject of linguistic

representation from another angle--as the source of non-mathematical models for linguistic science--and with another set of tools--the concepts of the philosophy of science and the principles of graphic design.

[26] Jespersen uses a directed graph as early as 1937:

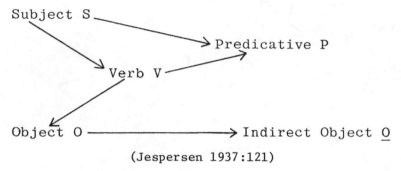

(Jespersen 1937:121)

Bibliography

Abercrombie, David. 1948. "Forgotten phoneticians."
  Transactions of the Philological Society 1948. 1-34.

Allen, W. Sidney. 1953. *Phonetics in ancient India*.
  London: Oxford University Press.

Anderson, Donald M. 1961. *Elements of design*. New York:
  Holt, Rinehart and Winston.

Anderson, John M. 1971a. "Dependency and grammatical
  functions." *Foundations of language* 7.30-37.

_____. 1971b. *The grammar of case: Towards a
  localistic theory*. Cambridge: Cambridge University
  Press.

Anttila, Raimo. 1972. *An introduction to historical and
  comparative linguistics*. New York: Macmillan.

Arnheim, Rudolf. 1964. *Art and visual perception*.
  Berkeley and Los Angeles: University of California
  Press.

_____. 1969. *Visual thinking*. Berkeley and Los
  Angeles: University of California Press.

Austerlitz, Robert. 1959. "Semantic components of
  pronoun systems: Gilyak." *Word* 15.102-109.

Austin, William M. 1957. "Criteria for phonetic
  similarity." *Language* 33.538-544.

Barnes, J. A. 1967. "Genealogies." *The craft of social
  anthropology*, ed. by A. L. Epstein, 101-127. London:
  Social Science Paperbacks.

Beckner, Morton. 1959. "Models in biological theory."
   The biological way of thought, ch. 3. New York:
   Columbia University Press.

Bell, Alexander M. 1867. *Visible speech*. London:
   Simpkin, Marshall; London and New York: N. Trubner.

Bever, Thomas G., and Peter S. Rosenbaum. 1970. "Some
   lexical structures and their empirical validity."
   Readings in English transformational grammar, ed.
   by Roderick A. Jacobs and Peter S. Rosenbaum, 3-19.
   Waltham, Mass.: Ginn and Company.

Black, Max. 1962. "Models and archetypes." *Models
   and metaphors: Studies in language and philosophy*,
   ch. 13. Ithaca, N.Y.: Cornell University Press.

Bloomfield, Leonard. 1929. Review of *Konkordanz Pāṇini-
   Candra*, by Bruno Liebich. *Language* 5.267-276.

_____. 1933. *Language*. New York: Holt, Rinehart
   and Winston.

Braithwaite, Richard B. 1953. "Models for scientific
   theories: their use and misuse." *Scientific
   explanation*, ch. 4. Cambridge: The University
   Press.

Bronowski, Jacob. 1965. "The discovery of form."
   Structure in art and science, ed. by Gyorgy Kepes,
   55-65. New York: Braziller.

_____. 1969. *Nature and knowledge*. Eugene, Oregon:
   University of Oregon Press.

Cairns, Charles E. 1972. Review of *Principles of
   phonology*, by Nicolai Sergeevich Trubetzkoy, tr.
   by Christiane M. Baltaxe. *Language* 47.918-931.

Campbell, Norman. 1921. *What is science?* London:
   Methuen.

Chao, Yuen Ren. 1962. "Models in linguistics and models
   in general." *Proceedings of the 1960 International
   Congress for Logic, Methodology, and Philosophy of
   Science*, ed. by Ernest Nagel, Patrick Suppes, and
   Alfred Tarski, 558-566. Stanford: Stanford
   University Press.

_____. 1968. *Language and symbolic systems*. Cambridge: Cambridge University Press.

Chapanes, Alphonse. 1963. "Men, machines, and models." *Theories in contemporary psychology*, ed. by Melvin H. Marx, 104-129. New York: Macmillan; London: Collier-Macmillan.

Chomsky, Noam. 1957. *Syntactic structures*. (Janua linguarum, 4). The Hague: Mouton.

_____. 1965. *Aspects of the theory of syntax*. Cambridge, Mass.: M. I. T. Press.

_____. 1970. "Remarks on nominalization." *Readings in English transformational grammar*, ed. by Roderick A. Jacobs and Peter S. Rosenbaum, 184-221. Waltham, Mass.: Ginn and Company.

_____, and Morris Halle. 1968. *The sound pattern of English*. New York: Harper & Row.

Colby, Benjamin N. 1966. "Ethnographic semantics: A preliminary survey." *Current anthropology* 7.3-32.

Conklin, Harold C. 1964. "Ethnogenealogical method." *Explorations in cultural anthropology: Essays in honor of George Peter Murdock*, ed. by Ward H. Goodenough, 25-55. New York: McGraw-Hill.

Cramer, Frank. 1896. *The method of Darwin: A study in scientific method*. Chicago: A. C. McClurg.

Darwin, Charles. 1859. *On the origin of species by means of natural selection, or The preservation of favored races in the struggle for life*. Facsimile rpt. Cambridge, Mass.: Harvard University Press, 1964.

Darwin, Francis (ed.). 1888. *The life and letters of Charles Darwin*, II. London: John Murray.

Emonds, Joseph E. 1970. "Root and structure-preserving transformations." M. I. T. doctoral dissertation.

Fillmore, Charles J. 1968. "The case for case." *Universals in linguistic theory*, ed. by Emmon Bach and Robert T. Harms, 1-88. New York: Holt, Rinehart and Winston.

Forchhammer, Jörgen. 1924. *Die Grundlage der Phonetik*. Heidelberg: Carl Winter.

Francis, W. Nelson. 1958. *The structure of American English*. New York: Ronald.

Fries, Charles C. 1952. *The structure of English: An introduction to the construction of English sentences*. New York: Harcourt, Brace & World.

Gentilhomme, Yves. 1969. "Propos sur l'utilisation des cadres formels en linguistique." *Linguistica antverpiensia* 3.81-100.

Gleason, H. A., Jr. 1961. *An introduction to descriptive linguistics*. Rev. ed. New York: Holt, Rinehart and Winston.

_____. 1965. *Linguistics and English grammar*. New York: Holt, Rinehart and Winston.

Gombrich, E. M. 1961. *Art and illusion*. 2nd ed. Princeton: Princeton University Press.

Goodman, Nelson. 1961. "Graphs for linguistics." *Structure of language and its mathematical aspects*, 51-55. Proceedings of Symposia in Applied Mathematics, XII. Providence: American Mathematical Society.

Greenberg, Joseph H. 1957. "Language and evolutionary theory." *Essays in linguistics*, 56-65. Chicago: University of Chicago Press.

Gregg, John R. 1954. *The language of taxonomy: An application of symbolic logic to the study of classificatory systems*. New York: Columbia University Press.

Hadamard, Jacques. 1945. *An essay on the psychology of invention in the mathematical field*. Princeton: Princeton University Press.

Halle, Morris. 1959. *The sound pattern of Russian*. The Hague: Mouton.

Harré, Romano. 1960. "Metaphor, model and mechanism." *Proceedings of the Aristotelian society* 60.101-122.

Hays, David G. 1964. "Dependency theory: A formalism and some observations." *Language* 40.511-525.

Herzberger, Hans G. 1961. "The joints of English." *Structure of language and its mathematical aspects*, 99-103. Proceedings of Symposia in Applied Mathematics, XII. Providence: American Mathematical Society.

Hesse, Mary B. 1966. *Models and analogies in science*. Notre Dame, Ind.: University of Notre Dame Press.

Hilbert, David, and S. Cohn-Vossen. 1952. *Geometry and the imagination*, tr. by P. Nemenyi. New York: Chelsea.

Hockett, Charles F. 1947. "Two models of grammatical description." *Word* 10.210-234.

_____. 1958. *A course in modern linguistics*. New York: Macmillan.

Holden, Alan. 1971. *Shapes, space, and symmetry*. New York and London: Columbia University Press.

Hoenigswald, Henry M. 1950. "Morpheme order diagrams." *Studies in linguistics* 8.79-81.

_____. 1963. "On the history of the comparative method." *Anthropological linguistics* 5/1.1-11.

Holton, Gerald. 1964. "Presupposition in the construction of theories." *Science as a cultural force*, ed. by Harry Woolf, 77-108. Baltimore: Johns Hopkins.

_____. 1965. "Conveying science by visual presentation." *The education of vision*, ed. by Gyorgy Kepes, 50-77. New York: Braziller.

Hudson, R. A. 1971. *English complex sentences: An introduction to systemic grammar*. New York: North-Holland.

Jakobson, Roman. 1936. "Beitrag zur allgemeinen Kasuslehre." *Travaux du Cercle linguistique de Prague* 6.240-288.

_____. 1957. *Shifters, verbal categories, and the Russian verb*. Cambridge, Mass.: Harvard University, Department of Slavic Languages and Literatures.

_____. 1958. "Morfologičeskie nabljudenija nad slavjanskim skloneniem (Sostav russkix padežnyx from)."

American contributions to the Fourth International Congress of Slavists, 127–156. The Hague: Mouton.

_____, and John Lotz. 1949. "Notes on the French phonemic pattern." *Word* 5.151–158.

Jespersen, Otto. 1889. *The articulations of speech sounds represented by means of analphabetic symbols*. Marburg: N. G. Elwert.

_____. 1934. *Modersmålets fonetik*. 3rd ed. Copenhagen: Gyldendalske.

_____. 1937. *Analytic syntax*. New York: Holt, Rinehart and Winston, 1969.

Joos, Martin. 1964. *The English verb. Form and meanings*. 1st ed. Madison: University of Wisconsin Press.

Kaplan, Abraham. 1964. *The conduct of inquiry: Methodology for behavioral science*. Scranton, Pa.: Chandler.

Katičić, Radoslav. 1966. "Modellbegriffe in der vergleichenden Sprachwissenschaft." *Kratylos* 12.49–67.

Katz, Jerrold J., and Paul M. Postal. 1964. *An integrated theory of linguistic descriptions*. Cambridge, Mass.: M. I. T. Press.

Kay, Paul. 1969. "Comments on Colby." *Cognitive anthropology*, ed. by Stephen A. Tyler, 78–90. New York: Holt.

_____. 1970. "On taxonomy and semantic contrasts." University of California Language Behavior Research Laboratory, working paper no. 31. (Also in *Language* 47.866–887.)

_____, and A. Kimball Romney. 1967. "On simple semantic spaces and semantic categories." University of California Language Behavior Research Laboratory, working paper no. 2.

Kepes, Gyorgy. 1944. *The language of vision*. Chicago: Theobald.

King, Robert D. 1967. "Push chains and drag chains." *Glossa* 3.3–21.

Klee, Paul. 1961. *Paul Klee: The thinking eye. The notebooks of Paul Klee*, ed. by Jürg Spiller, tr. by Ralph Manheim. New York: Wittenborn.

Kuhn, Thomas. 1962. *The structure of scientific revolutions. International Encyclopedia of Unified Science* 2/2. Chicago: University of Chicago Press.

Lachman, Roy. 1963. "The model in theory construction." *Theories in contemporary psychology*, ed. by Melvin H. Marx, 78-89. New York: Macmillan; London: Collier-Macmillan.

Lakoff, George. 1970. *Irregularity in syntax*. New York: Holt, Rinehart and Winston.

Lamarck, Jean Baptiste P.-A. 1809. *Philosophie zoologique*. Facsimile rpt. Historiae Naturalis Classica 10 (1960).

Lamb, Sydney M. 1966. *Outline of stratificational grammar*. Washington, D. C.: Georgetown University Press.

Lockwood, Arthur. 1969. *Diagrams: A visual survey of graphs, maps, charts and diagrams for the graphic designer*. London: Studio Vista Limited; New York: Watson-Guptill.

Lotz, John. 1967. "Numerical properties of linguistic structures." *Anthropological linguistics* 9/4.1-4.

Lyons, John. 1968. *Introduction to theoretical linguistics*. Cambridge: Cambridge University Press.

Maas, Paul. 1957. *Textkritik*. 3rd ed. Leipzig: B. G. Teubner.

Maher, John P. 1966. "More on the history of the comparative method: The tradition of Darwinism in August Schleicher's work." *Anthropological linguistics* 8/3 (pt. 2).1-12.

Martinet, André. 1955. *Economie des changements phonétiques: Traité de phonologie diachronique*. Bern: Francke.

Modley, Rudolf. 1966. "Graphic symbols for world-wide communication." *Sign, image, symbol*, ed. by Gyorgy Kepes, 108-125. New York: Braziller.

Morin, Yves Ch., and Michael O'Malley. 1969. "Multi-rooted vines in semantic representation." *Papers from the fifth regional meeting, Chicago Linguistic Society*, 178–185. Chicago: University of Chicago Department of Linguistics.

Moulton, William G. 1962. "Dialect geography and the concept of phonological space." *Word* 18.23–32.

_____. MS. "Two models for phonology."

Nagel, Ernest. 1961. *The structure of science: Problems in the logic of scientific explanation*. New York: Harcourt.

Nida, Eugene A. 1964. *Toward a science of translating*. Leiden: Brill.

_____. 1966. *A synopsis of English syntax*. 2nd ed. The Hague: Mouton.

Ong, Walter J., S. J. 1958. *Ramus: Method and the decay of dialogue*. Cambridge, Mass.: Harvard University Press.

Ore, Oystein. 1963. *Graphs and their uses*. New York: Random House.

Pfalz, Anton. 1918. "Reihenschritte im Vokalismus." *Beiträge zur Kunde der bayerisch-österreichischen Mundarten*, ch. 2. Akademie der Wissenschaften in Wien, Philosophisch-historische Klasse, Sitzungsberichte 190/2.

Pike, Kenneth L. 1943. *Phonetics: A critical analysis of phonetic theory and a technic for the practical description of sounds*. Ann Arbor: University of Michigan Press; Don Mills, Canada: Longmans Canada.

_____. 1947. *Phonemics: A technique for reducing languages to writing*. Ann Arbor: University of Michigan Press.

_____. 1959. "Language as particle, wave, and field." *Texas quarterly* 2/2.37–54.

_____. 1962. "Dimensions of grammatical constructions." *Language* 38.221–224.

_____, and Barbara Erickson. 1964. "Conflated field structures in Potawatomi and Arabic." *International journal of American linguistics* 30.201-212.

Postal, Paul M. 1971. *Cross-over phenomena*. New York: Holt, Rinehart and Winston, Inc.

Revzin, Isaak I. 1966. *Models of language*, tr. by N. F. C. Owen and A. S. C. Ross. London: Methuen.

Robinson, Jane J. 1970a. "Case, category and configuration." *Journal of linguistics* 6/1.57-80.

_____. 1970b. "Dependency structures and transformational rules." *Language* 46/2 (part I).259-285.

Rosenblueth, Arturo, and Norbert Wiener. 1945. "The role of models in science." *Philosophy of science* 12.316-321.

Ross, John Robert. 1967. "Constraints on variables in syntax." M. I. T. doctoral dissertation.

_____. 1969. "A proposed rule of tree-pruning." *Modern studies in English: Readings in transformational grammar*, ed. by David A. Reibel and Sanford A. Schane, 288-299. Englewood Cliffs, N.J.: Prentice-Hall.

Saussure, Ferdinand de. 1879. *Mémoire sur le système primitif des voyelles dans les langues indo-européenes*. Leipzig: B. G. Teubner.

_____. 1916. *Cours de linguistique générale*, ed. by Charles Bally and Albert Sechehaye. 3rd ed. Paris: Payot, 1931.

Schleicher, August. 1888. *Die deutsche Sprache*. 5th ed. Stuttgart: J. G. Cotta'schen.

Schmidt, Johannes. 1872. *Verwandschaftsverhältnisse der indogermanischen Sprachen*. Weimar: Hermann Bölau.

Schrader, Otto von. 1883. *Sprachvergleichung und Ur- geschichte: Linguistisch-historische Beiträge zur Erforschung des indogermanischen Altertums*. Jena: Hermann Castenoble.

Scott, Robert G. 1951. *Design fundamentals*. New York: McGraw-Hill.

Sebeok, Thomas A. 1946. *Finnish and Hungarian case systems:
    Their form and function*. Acta Instituti Hungarici
    Universitatis Holmiensis, Series B. Linguistica 3.

Sievers, Eduard. 1881. *Grundzüge der Lautphysiologie zur
    Einfuhrung in das Studium der Lautlehre der indo-
    germanischen Sprachen*. 2nd ed. Leipzig: Breitkopf
    and Härtel.

Simpson, George Gaylord. 1961. *Principles of animal
    taxonomy*. New York: Columbia University Press.

Southworth, Franklin C. 1964. "Family-tree diagrams."
    Language 40.557-565.

Stevick, Robert D. 1963. "The biological model and
    historical linguistics." *Language* 39.159-169.

Stockwell, Robert P., Paul Schachter, and Barbara Hall
    Partee. 1973. *The major syntactic structures of
    English*. New York: Holt, Rinehart and Winston.

Svensen, Carl Lars. 1935. *Drafting for engineers: A
    textbook of engineering drawing for colleges and
    technical schools*. 2nd ed. New York: Van Nostrand.

Sweet, Henry. 1890. *A primer of phonetics*. Oxford:
    Clarendon.

Tesnière, Lucien. 1959. *Eléments de syntaxe structurale*.
    Paris: C. Klincksieck.

Toulmin, Stephen. 1953. *The philosophy of science*. Rpt.
    New York: Harper & Row.

Trager, George L., and Henry Lee Smith, Jr. 1950. "A
    chronology of Indo-Hittite." *Studies in linguistics*
    8.61-69.

Trubetzkoy, Nicolai S. 1939. *Grundzüge der Phonologie*.
    Prague: Cercle linguistique de Prague.

Voegelin, Charles F. 1959. "Model-directed structurali-
    zation." *Anthropological linguistics* 1/1.9-25.

Von Ostermann, George F., and A. E. Giegengack. 1936.
    *Manual of foreign languages for the use of printers
    and translators*. 3rd ed. Washington, D. C.:
    Government Printing Office.

Walkup, Lewis E. 1965. "Creativity in science through
    visualization." *Perceptual and motor skills* 21.35-41.

Wallace, Anthony F. C., and John Atkins. 1960. "The
    meaning of kinship terms." *American anthropologist*
    62.58-80.

Watkins, C. Law. 1946. *The language of design*.
    Washington, D. C.: Phillips Memorial Gallery.

Weinreich, Uriel. 1966. "Explorations in semantic theory."
    Current trends in linguistics, ed. by Thomas A. Sebeok,
    III, 395-477. The Hague: Mouton.

Weyl, Hermann. 1952. *Symmetry*. Princeton: Princeton
    University Press.

Whitney, William Dwight. 1889. *Sanskrit grammar, including
    the classical language and the older dialects, of Veda
    and Brahmana*. 2nd ed., 11th issue. Cambridge, Mass.:
    Harvard University Press.

Yngve, Victor H. 1960. "A model and an hypothesis for
    language structure." *Proceedings of the American
    Philosophical Society* 104.444-466.

Zierer, Ernesto. 1970. *The theory of graphs in linguistics*.
    (Janua linguarum, 94.) The Hague: Mouton.

Index

Abercrombie, David, 42
Allen, W. Sidney, 39–41,
169n5
Analphabetic notation, 42–44
See also Bell, Alexander
Melville; Jespersen, Otto;
Sweet, Henry; Universal
alphabet
Anderson, Donald M., 109,
171n17, 172n18
Anderson, John M., 143,
171n16, 172n21
Anttila, Raimo, 116, 117
Arnheim, Rudolf, 108
Art elements: movement, 91–
92, 94–95, 103, 126, 155;
hue, 103; intensity, 103;
texture, 103; shape, 103–4,
112; line, 103, 112, 114,
118, 128; space, 103, 112,
114, 128; value, 103, 112,
130–31; listed, 103, 112,
171n17; volume, 103, 153;
expressive value of, 108–9,
112; in linguistics, 118
Articulatory phonetics: and
devanāgarī alphabet, 41;
and matrix, 41, 48, 82, 83;
and three-dimensional
models, 161, 164–6. *See
also* Features, phonetic;

Phonological space
Atkins, John, 126
Austerlitz, Robert, 63, 140
Austin, William: theory of
sound change, 86–88, 92,
126

Barnes, J. A., 7
Beckner, Morton, 170n9
Bell, Alexander Melville:
Visible Speech, 2, 42–43;
analphabetic notation of,
42–43, 46; and universal
alphabet, 43, 46
Bever, Thomas G., 26–27, 34,
148–49
Black, Max, 80, 169n8, 170n9,
170n10, 170n11
Bloomfield, Leonard, 16, 17;
subcategorization of Eng-
lish nouns, 22, 23; on
disadvantages of compara-
tive method, 100
Braithwaite, Richard B.,
169–70n8, 170n10
Bronowski, Jacob, 17, 19

Cairns, Charles E., 85
Campbell, Norman, 78, 169n8,
170n10
Case grammar, 171n16; tree